NEW DIRECTIONS FOR COMMUNITY COLLEGES

Arthur M. Cohen
EDITOR-IN-CHIEF

Florence B. Brawer
ASSOCIATE EDITOR

Preparing Department Chairs for Their Leadership Roles

Rosemary Gillett-Karam
Louisburg College

EDITOR

Number 105, Spring 1999

JOSSEY-BASS PUBLISHERS
San Francisco

ERIC®

Clearinghouse for Community Colleges

PREPARING DEPARTMENT CHAIRS FOR THEIR LEADERSHIP ROLES
Rosemary Gillett-Karam (ed.)
New Directions for Community Colleges, no. 105
Volume XXVII, number 1
Arthur M. Cohen, Editor-in-Chief
Florence B. Brawer, Associate Editor

New Directions for Community Colleges is indexed in Current Index to
Journals in Education (ERIC).

Microfilm copies of issues and articles are available in 16mm and 35mm,
as well as microfiche in 105mm, through University Microfilms Inc., 300
North Zeeb Road, Ann Arbor, Michigan 48106–1346.

ISSN 0194-3081   ISBN 0-7879-4846-2

NEW DIRECTIONS FOR COMMUNITY COLLEGES is part of The Jossey-Bass
Higher and Adult Education Series and is published quarterly by Jossey-
Bass Inc., Publishers, 350 Sansome Street, San Francisco, California
94104–1342, in association with the ERIC Clearinghouse for Community
Colleges. Periodicals postage paid at San Francisco, California, and at
additional mailing offices. POSTMASTER: Send address changes to New
Directions for Community Colleges, Jossey-Bass Inc., Publishers, 350 San-
some Street, San Francisco, California 94104–1342.

SUBSCRIPTIONS cost $57.00 for individuals and $107.00 for institutions,
agencies, and libraries. Prices subject to change.

THE MATERIAL in this publication is based on work sponsored wholly or
in part by the Office of Educational Research and Improvement, U.S.
Department of Education, under contract number RI-93-00-2003. Its contents do not necessarily reflect the views of the Department or any other
agency of the U.S. Government.

EDITORIAL CORRESPONDENCE should be sent to the Editor-in-Chief, Arthur
M. Cohen, at the ERIC Clearinghouse for Community Colleges, University of California, 3051 Moore Hall, Box 951521, Los Angeles, California
90095–1521. All manuscripts receive anonymous reviews by external ref-
erees.

Cover photograph © Rene Sheret, After Image, Los Angeles, California,
1990.

www.josseybass.com

Printed in the United States of America on acid-free recycled paper con-
taining 100 percent recovered waste paper, of which at least 20 percent is
postconsumer waste.

Contents

Editor's Notes

The department head at the community college may also be known by other titles, such as department chair, division chair, division dean, or academic dean. This position is considered to be the front line in community college administration. Department heads are managers and leaders who are internally responsible for the day-to-day operation of the college. In charge of academic departments, divisions, or programs, the chair (a compromise title) is the quintessential manager or leader from the middle level of administration who deals with curricula and program review and change; faculty hiring, development, evaluation, and scheduling; student satisfaction with curriculum and faculty; student complaints, grievances, and success; and budget and planning analyses. Additionally, chairs act as liaisons and representatives to staff, upper-level administration, and the community. Thought of as the glue that binds together students, faculty, curriculum, and college, the chair rarely acts as a free agent. Rather, he or she is a representative of the institution to its constituencies.

The complexity of the midlevel manager's job has been addressed by many previous studies of this position. Recognizing that complexity, this volume posits the need for midlevel managers to learn about and train for this unique administrative job and leadership role in the community college. In the various chapters, university professors, college presidents, and practitioners offer insight into the roles and needs of the midlevel manager in community colleges today. Specifically, the authors respond to the need for learning and training for leaders at this administrative level. They describe several existing options for learning and training, and offer insight into the changing nature of midlevel management and leadership as we approach a new century.

In Chapter One I address the question, Is midlevel management needed in community colleges today? The question is reviewed in light of current trends in the business world, where midlevel management is being reduced and organizations are being restructured. The need for training and professional development is influenced by such contextual factors. This chapter illustrates how a credit-earning university program for current and potential community college chairs can develop the skills necessary for management at the midlevel. The program focuses on five core areas for chair training: leadership, scholarship, research and application, teamwork and collaboration, and skills.

In Chapter Two, Robin L. Spaid and Michael H. Parsons, two administrators from Hagerstown Community College, address the need for midlevel managers to respond to current and impending organizational change. According to a new leadership paradigm, leaders will need to focus on releasing human potential, balancing individual and group needs, defining values, and instilling initiative and responsibility if institutions are to prosper in the new millennium. The key to leadership is communication, and the overall goal is to foster shared meaning, understanding, and commitment. On the basis of these emerging leadership concepts, Spaid and Parsons conducted a study of midlevel administrators at community colleges and a regional hospital. Both groups of managers indicated that honesty and learning from mistakes were their critical values. These midlevel managers agreed that teamwork is essential to effective administration. Furthermore, they also agreed to learn to lead from where they currently are.

An example of a district-based administrative training program is given in Chapter Three. Mary S. Spangler, president of Los Angeles City College, describes the creation, function, and administrative development concept of the Administrative Leadership Institute (ALI) for staff of the Los Angeles Community College District. Recognizing the need for midlevel management development, the ALI program seeks to cultivate future administrators from among current college personnel. Drawing from various learning and training models, the ALI attempts to offer training and development programs that utilize internal sources in order to serve organizational vision, mission, and principles better.

In Chapter Four, Albert B. Smith and Gloria A. Stewart share their findings from a study of fifty-nine new department chairs in Texas. The chairs were asked how they prepared for their jobs, what they encountered on the job, and how they adapted their jobs to the challenges they did not or could not anticipate. Role transitioning or socialization forms the theoretical basis for understanding this study. Not surprisingly, new chairs had little formal training for their jobs and had to rely on past experience or observation to guide their practices. They were unprepared for the amount of administrative tasks involved in being the chair, and the most often cited method of learning the job was "doing the job." Smith and Stewart demonstrate that these new chairs were seeking formal training for their jobs.

In Chapter Five, six community college presidents—Donald W. Cameron, Robert C. Messina, Jr., Stephen K. Mittelstet, Anne E. Mulder, Abel B. Sykes, Jr., and Jerry Sue Thornton—respond to questions about midlevel managers on their campuses. These top-level administrators provide definitions of midlevel management and descriptions of duties, opinions about the necessity and efficacy of midlevel managers, and examples of the successes of current midlevel administrators at their institutions. All of these presidents agree that there is a need for this position in the community college. Also, all six view effective communication on the job as the midlevel manager's top skill.

Gary L. Filan, executive director of Maricopa's Chair Academy, is the author of Chapter Six. He describes the development of the Chair Academy from a grassroots movement in early 1990 to an organization that now sponsors a full-fledged national conference. By highlighting exemplary practices of chairs in community colleges nationwide, the academy offers two training routes for present and future community college midlevel administrators. First, the weeklong annual conference provides a chance to learn from and share with others through symposia, roundtables, and networking. The Chair Academy also provides administrators with the opportunity to engage in a three-year practicum and training program for chair development. Furthermore, the academy has benefited from the results of a national study on chairs' training needs and is beginning to offer college credit courses on-line for midlevel management training.

We have been apprised and reminded by several of the authors of this volume that chairs and midlevel managers generally learn their job on the job. In Chapter Seven, John M. Pettitt honors this tradition as an excellent example of adult education practices. Situated learning is such a practice in which role, relationship, and legitimate participation are derived from actual activities engaged in on the job—that is, learning by doing the things chairs do. Data are given that demonstrate characteristics of North Carolina department chairs, and a model for implementing situated learning is offered. Learning can be self-directed and efficient; situated learning demonstrates this from the perspective of learning by doing.

In Chapter Eight, Erika Yamasaki considers the challenge facing chairs who not only juggle their conflicting academic and administrative roles but also desire to be leaders. As the literature indicates, successful management does not necessarily constitute effective leadership. Therefore, those who strive to be managerial leaders must provide departmental vision, empower colleagues and staff, and foster shared values in addition to fulfilling their administrative duties. Emerging leadership models provide some guidance for chairs as they pursue this formidable task.

Finally, in Chapter Nine, Elizabeth Foote of the ERIC Clearinghouse for Community Colleges describes various studies of the chair position not included in the preceding chapters. She also provides an overview of leadership training programs designed for community college chairs.

Rosemary Gillett-Karam
Editor

ROSEMARY GILLETT-KARAM is president, Louisburg College, Louisburg, North Carolina.

Recognizing that the duties and responsibilities of the department chair in the community college are quite complex, North Carolina State University developed a training program for practitioners.

Midlevel Management in the Community College: A Rose Garden?

Rosemary Gillett-Karam

There's a good ol' country-and-western classic called "I Never Promised You a Rose Garden" in which Lynn Anderson attempts to point out the struggles and expectations that relationships create. She could very well be talking about midlevel management in community colleges. This job is all about relationships, and it too doesn't promise a rose garden.

Although chairs are considered administrators, they really are not. They are also considered faculty, but they are not really. Although they are considered leaders, they are usually managers whose job descriptions, roles, and duties are bound to traditional hierarchical organizational structures. Though not priests, psychologists, accountants, or lawyers, chairs act in these roles. Thought to be riding the wave to the top, chairs are more often in a holding pattern and not in line for advancement to high-level administration. Gmelch and Miskin (1993) and Tucker (1993) report that four of every five chairs never move up the administrative ladder. Furthermore, burnout and stress are occupational hazards of this job that frequently takes a toll on individuals' personal lives, health, and outside commitments.

The understandably complex position of department chair links students to faculty, faculty to administration, and people to the organization. Long considered the buffer between faculty and administration, the chair is more a mediator, communicator, and facilitator than any of the conventional descriptors bestowed on leaders by the literature. The chair is ever present and often considered the key administrator who resides over daily college affairs.

Institutional success parallels that of the chair's success, because without the chair's sense of timing, direction, skills, and leadership, the college stands to lose its cohesiveness, alignment, and representation. Unlike upper-level administrators who are responsible to various external constituencies, the chair's attention is focused internally on the day-to-day administration of the campus. Upper-level administration is expected to declare the vision and mission of the college, but without coordination and cooperation between upper-level administrators and chairs who are aligned with students and faculty, the vision and mission of the college would not be well grounded or representative. Acting as the conduit for faculty and student concerns is not the only role of the chair, however.

Researchers have spent the last thirty years trying to understand the critical role of the chair in both university and community college settings. Scheufler (1973) suggests that the chair performs as many as 113 specific tasks; Lombardi (1974) lists fifty-one duties; Tucker (1984) names fifty-five. Seagren and others (1994) asked community college chairs to respond to 190 questions pertaining to chair responsibilities. Generally, research on chairs and midlevel managers in higher education addresses the question, What kind of person can develop expertise in overseeing curriculum issues, hiring and firing, resolving student complaints, mediating disputes among faculty, managing a budget, facilitating community relations, understanding the legal implications of lawsuits, administering policy, and being a participative and collaborative leader? Furthermore, what kind of a person can do these jobs as a team player both with upper-level administration and among faculty, staff, students, and community groups? Researchers agree that the chair's role is difficult and that leading from the middle is no easy task (Gmelch and Miskin, 1995; Hickson and Stacks, 1992; Seagren and others, 1994; Lucas, 1994).

The refrain from "I Never Promised You a Rose Garden" provides some indication of what is needed to accomplish the duties, tasks, and responsibilities of the chair. Anderson warns us that often there are individual costs associated with the risks we take. To heed this warning, chairs need to be trained to gauge the depth of the waters and to look before they leap. Learning through practice and continuing to reflect while on the job are the cornerstones of this training process. Therefore, colleges and universities whose departments and faculty provide administrative leadership training should certainly consider extending training to midlevel managers and leaders.

At North Carolina State University (NCSU), faculty took on this challenge three years ago by offering current and potential community college chairs and division deans an opportunity to develop their leadership skills. A needs assessment revealed that most college chairs rarely received any training for their complex positions. This information prompted NCSU faculty to work cooperatively with the state community college system to develop a statewide program for practitioners.

North Carolina community college presidents nominated and paid faculty from their colleges to engage in six hours of credit-earning training from NCSU. Certification was guaranteed through the North Carolina Community College System. In weekend classes lasting two semesters, chairs and potential chairs worked to learn leadership and organizational skills appropriate to midlevel management positions. During the second semester, students interned with seasoned chairs. Both in the classroom and in an experiential setting, students were able to study, observe, practice, and make (and correct) mistakes before they moved into midlevel management positions. One student commented, "I never realized the enormity of the job; no wonder the majority of chairs return to faculty positions after their tenure is over."

Development Model

Chair training in the NCSU program is designed to help managers and other practitioners broaden their knowledge as well as their midlevel supervision and management skills. Training also helps them apply leadership concepts, practices, and processes, especially as they relate to the needs of actual work situations. To develop effective management and leadership skills, the program emphasizes five training areas: leadership, scholarship, research and application, teamwork and collaboration, and skill development.

Leadership. This core skill requires the acquisition and further understanding of patterns, competencies, behaviors, traits, personality, and orientations both of leadership in general and in one's own leadership practice. This recognition of personal leadership style and practice is the subject of group analyses as well. Understanding the responsibilities, roles, strategies, and aspirations of midlevel managers is key to learning to be a successful leader. Relative to upper-level leadership, leading from the middle is more hands-on and duties are less easy to delegate. The chair is instrumental in motivating, evaluating, rewarding, and providing faculty development. When these efforts are deficient in an institution, the chair is responsible. As a communicator, the chair is a listener, an interpreter, a memo writer, a planner of meetings, and a fair and impartial mediator. The chair does all this communication up, down, and laterally in the organization. As a planner, the chair integrates the college's vision and mission into his or her academic area. As a survivor, the chair is resilient to the unexpected while also maintaining a healthy college climate. To facilitate a deeper understanding of this leadership concept, the training program reviews traditional styles of leadership, the power of leaders, interpersonal skills, ethical leadership, and new models of leadership and work.

Teamwork and collaboration. It is expected that the participants, working in the NCSU program's team setting, will develop several useful documents and practices for implementation at their individual institutions. If institutions are to become more learning centered rather than teaching centered, collaboration among various levels of administrative strata is expected. Clearly, neither a single dictate nor a single department can affect the entire institution. Collaboration requires learning to work in teams; handling conflict resolution; making decisions through a broad, ethical process; and expecting political roadblocks. The conventional wisdom among business gurus is that midlevel managers are best suited to organize and develop productive, efficient teams.

Scholarship. Practitioners require an intellectual base in which to ground their understanding of organizations and leadership responsibilities. Therefore the training program's emphasis in this area requires acquiring and understanding the major research and theoretical developments in midlevel management and supervision, especially those relating to the chair as an organizational leader, and including the more obvious discipline-specific knowledge. Scholarship's pursuit, its relationships to other disciplines, its application to the issues of present social reality, and its relevance to the active learning of the student are all chair responsibilities. Furthermore, once thought of as senior-institution tasks, publishing and grant writing are also the responsibility of chairs in community colleges.

Research and application. Practitioners are required to develop proficiency in selecting, integrating, and applying appropriate concepts from social and behavioral science and adult education in formulating and implementing approaches to management and supervisory problems and issues. Organizational studies that employ learning and critical theories, rather than traditional structure and function approaches, are often utilized for this purpose. Observing and acting "outside the box" requires practitioners to question present expectations and norms assigned to the midlevel manager. By becoming reflective thinkers, practitioners can evaluate the effectiveness of practices and results. Additionally, they can establish research-based practices that are more meaningful to their work, their discipline, and their college.

Skill development. Although all the concepts already mentioned require skills, the area of skill development specifically addresses those skills that are essential to practitioners' job and role effectiveness. Practitioners develop skills in conflict management and mediation, making presentations, oral and written communication, team building, policy interpretation, liability and legal implications, change, and stress reduction. Case studies that most closely represent situations and issues in the workplace are used as learning tools.

Training

The fundamental expectation of the chair training program is that all work will be accomplished collaboratively. Early on, participants are assigned to several affinity groups. As an introductory exercise, they work together without using words to define the roles, responsibilities, and job descriptions of the chair. This team-building activity emphasizes that each individual's ideas are important and thereby leads the way to further teamwork and team learning. The exercise also frames leadership as a team responsibility in which experience-based learners are expected to discover and practice the interconnectivity between leadership and personal relationships.

Participants also examine current research on chairs (such as Seagren and others, 1994; Gmelch and Miskin, 1995; Hilton, 1997), especially those studies that concentrate on the roles of chairs in colleges and universities. Participants also administer questionnaires. Meeting in teams to discuss the pluses and minuses of the questionnaires used in the studies, each student interviews other class members to determine their views of departments and divisions they have known. Further questions are asked to assess present department or division needs, including the following:

How do you describe the strengths of your department (position)? Why are they considered strengths?

How do you describe the weaknesses of your department (position)? Why are they considered weaknesses?

What changes would you suggest to improve your department (position)? Why?

How well do the following terms describe your chair: leader, scholar, manager, faculty developer?

How would you delineate the use of time by your chair?

How effective is your chair? What criteria would you use to evaluate his or her effectiveness?

These questions aid practitioners in determining the perceptions not only of current chairs but also of their constituent groups, including faculty, students, community groups, and upper-level administrators.

Team learning is accomplished by using case scenarios designed by both students and the professor. After the case study method is reviewed in class, several scenarios of chairs' experiences are presented. By offering a nonpunitive setting for role-playing, some common issues affecting chairs can be played out with various outcomes. The cases can be replayed and reexamined as new issues arise.

Another team-learning method utilized in the program is benchmarking, a process that requires students to look at the best practices in the literature, on college and university campuses, and in business. Program participants must gather evidence from at least five institutions regarding their best practices for chairs. Guest speakers from both academic and business settings offer their expertise, experience, and advice to potential chairs.

Student teams also learn by examining and implementing various leadership skills in the areas of presentation and communication; hiring, firing, and retiring; curriculum; human relations; budgeting; legal and policy analysis; and mediation-facilitation. Current chairs, division chairs, deans, and presidents also share their experiences, offer advice, and provide work experiences for interns.

Shadowing a superior or other practitioner provides another training venue for program participants. This aspect of training is meant to provide a real-world experience in which the student is expected to become actively involved in the work and workplace of the mentor. The mentor and participant jointly decide on the project that will form the basis of the shadowing experience.

Finally, continuous evaluation of the training model constitutes a critical learning opportunity. Also important is discovering how the training program affects the work and lives of the trainees.

Conclusion

Anderson's song reminds us to smile through our difficulties and to find joy in what we do as leaders. Rose gardens, it seems, can recover from thunderstorms. And so can chairs. The "good times" are gleaned from insights and research into the modern midlevel manager at the community college. Recovery comes through professional development and training.

Professional development and training programs help future chairs to understand the leadership roles that will be expected of them, to recognize and make better use of decision making as a collaborative venture among equals, and to expect and participate in team building among the various constituencies in both the college and the community. In developing their skills, chairs also learn to put into practice the management skills of the chair. They are more than manipulators of paperwork (more than accountants, record holders, schedulers, report writers, formal evaluators, budget managers, executors of policy, and in general, information disseminators). They are also human relations experts, dealing with people issues, conflict, dilemmas, debate, and controversy. They are expected to be managers of human needs and wants, negotiators of interest groups, examiners of power relationships, mentors, and change agents. Finally, professional development and training prepare chairs to guide the college's academic disciplines and programs and the successes of faculty and students.

Chairs are currently the subject of attention from many groups, including those involved in organizational studies and business management who, in accordance with restructuring, rightsizing, downsizing, and bureaucratic layering adjustments, are questioning the need for midlevel management. Community colleges are also questioning the need for such positions, especially when the roles of faculty and administrator coincide and collide, as in peer evaluations in a union setting. In these situations, chairs have clearly become only administrators. Obviously where some colleges go, others will follow. But the refrain remains the same: chairs can provide the good times, and in doing so, allow the rose garden (or college) to prosper.

References

Gmelch, W., and Miskin, V. *Leadership Skills for Department Chairs*. Bolton, Mass.: Anker, 1993.
Gmelch, W., and Miskin, V. *Chairing an Academic Department*. Thousand Oaks, Calif.: Sage, 1995.
Hickson, M., and Stacks, D. *Effective Communication for Academic Chairs*. Albany: State University of New York, 1992.

Hilton, H. "Department Chairs' Roles, Functions, and Needs for Professional Development in North Carolina's Community Colleges." Unpublished doctoral dissertation, North Carolina State University, 1997.

Lombardi, J. *The Department/Division Chairman: Characteristics and Role in the Community College.* Topical paper no. 40. Los Angeles: ERIC Clearinghouse for Community Colleges, May 1974.

Lucas, A. *Strengthening Departmental Leadership: A Team-Building Guide for Chairs in Colleges and Universities.* San Francisco: Jossey-Bass, 1994.

Scheufler, A. "Roles and Responsibilities of Department Chairs." Unpublished doctoral dissertation, University of Tennessee, 1973.

Seagren, A. T., Wheeler, D. W., Creswell, J. W., Miller, M. T., and VanHorn-Grassmeyer, K. *Academic Leadership in Community Colleges.* Lincoln: University of Nebraska Press, 1994.

Tucker, A. *Chairing the Academic Department: Leaderhip Among Peers.* (2nd ed.) New York: ACE/Macmillan, 1984.

Tucker, A. *Chairing the Academic Department: Leadership Among Peers.* Phoenix: Oryx Press, 1993.

ROSEMARY GILLETT-KARAM is president, Louisburg College, Louisburg, North Carolina.

A new paradigm for leadership in the twenty-first century identifies essential elements for adapting to change: weaving a shared vision, appreciating a variety of views, communicating effectively, making decisions based on principles, and creating the future.

Meeting the Millennium's Challenge: Leading from Where You Are

Robin L. Spaid, Michael H. Parsons

As we completed the research for this article, fewer than five hundred days remained before the onset of the twenty-first century. Most futurists believe that the twenty-first century will be characterized as a new age of knowledge. Community college staff, working as community development agents, must design new sets of competencies necessary to reap the opportunities associated with a new paradigm (Norris, 1998). Change will be an integral part of the new century's challenge, but even change will be different. It will involve a complete break with traditional perception and require a major reconstruction of every aspect of an organization. If community colleges are to remain the people's colleges, they must depend on internal leadership to manage discontinuous change. Elements of this leadership will include adaptiveness, flexibility, responsiveness, and ethical sensitivity.

Half a century ago, Einstein indicated that "no problem can be solved from the same consciousness that created it. We must learn to see the world anew," (Wheatley, 1992, p. 5). A common theme that permeates futurists' analyses of the coming century is that hierarchical, top-down leadership will no longer suffice. It is imperative that people learn to lead from where they are. Middle management will play a significant role in changing the focus of leadership. In her synthesis of physical science principles and social change, Wheatley (1992) reminds us that people support what they create and recreate. As the leadership design changes, all participants will also change, through engagement with others and with technology, and through interaction with internal and external events. Clearly a new leadership focus will be essential in order for community colleges to continue their historic mission.

The Path of Leadership

The need for change in leadership has not gone unnoticed. A number of organizational analyses have begun to look at the nature of redesign. In their assessment of more than one hundred public and private sector organizations, Kline and Saunders (1998) identify as a critical benchmark the need for everyone in an organization to change if institutional redesign is to be productive.

The Kellogg Foundation funded a study conducted by the director of their Leadership Scholar Program. Larraine R. Matusak (1997) spent two years assessing components of leadership in an era of unprecedented, multifaceted change. Her findings suggest that critical incidents in leadership for the twenty-first century will include visioning, initiating, guiding, and encouraging with and through a group. Further, emergent leaders must have the courage to take the initiative that will translate a vision or passion into reality. Matusak's study identifies four core values that are essential if an organization is to prosper in the new social context (p. 21):

- Releasing human potential
- Balancing individual and group needs
- Defining and defending fundamental values throughout the internal and external community
- Instilling and facilitating initiative and responsibility at all organizational levels

Another interesting insight that Matusak provides is a reminder that leadership is situational. It is a process that requires moving from the role of leader to the role of follower, depending on circumstances. Finally, she identifies communication as the key to leadership. The process is multidimensional. Leaders must listen not only to what is being said but also to what is not being said. The overall goal is to create shared meaning, shared understanding, and shared commitment. This task is daunting. Where does an individual or an organization begin this journey without end? Matusak suggests that "everyone must take the initiative to discover personal strengths and assume responsibilities on whatever level one may find him or herself" (p. 21). Has the process begun? Behavioral scientists, as observers of human interaction, treat their observations as measurement techniques. The resulting trends are critical incidents in change management.

In an effort to determine what critical incidents are necessary for today's leaders, we developed an instrument (see Exhibit 2.1) and surveyed thirty-nine individuals. Our purpose was to study community college administrators at various levels by asking them to assess the importance of specific leadership behaviors and requesting that they report the extent to which they can be situational facilitators of organizational change. The concept of situational facilitators is based on the Hersey and Blanchard (1982) leadership design used by public and private sector organizations for more than thirty years.

Exhibit 2.1. Leadership Paradigm

This behavior is an essential element of leadership.

I am able to use this element in my position.

Very Important Important Neutral Less important Not important

1 2 3 4 5	Serving as a change agent	1 2 3 4 5
1 2 3 4 5	Being accessible to my constituents	1 2 3 4 5
1 2 3 4 5	Accepting the role of a follower	1 2 3 4 5
1 2 3 4 5	Serving as a catalyst for consensus	1 2 3 4 5
1 2 3 4 5	Being open to different ways of accomplishing old tasks	1 2 3 4 5
1 2 3 4 5	Promoting teamwork	1 2 3 4 5
1 2 3 4 5	Breaking down communication barriers	1 2 3 4 5
1 2 3 4 5	Convincing others that my point of view is correct	1 2 3 4 5
1 2 3 4 5	Accepting compromise as a means of achieving organizational goals	1 2 3 4 5
1 2 3 4 5	Being honest	1 2 3 4 5
1 2 3 4 5	Taking risks	1 2 3 4 5
1 2 3 4 5	Admitting mistakes	1 2 3 4 5
1 2 3 4 5	Learning from mistakes	1 2 3 4 5
1 2 3 4 5	Listening to all points of view	1 2 3 4 5

Please state in two or three sentences your approach to leadership:

_____

_____

_____

Source: Copyright © 1998 Robin L. Spaid.

The Practice of Leadership

Scholars are examining human behavior as it is affected by increasing change. In the past two decades a number of individuals have emerged as chroniclers of leadership behavior. In 1978, James MacGregor Burns published a landmark study on leadership. It drew on his study of the American presidency, translating critical incidents in presidential leadership into a broader organizational context.

Throughout the 1980s, Warren Bennis studied leaders in both the public and private sectors. Perhaps the most telling synthesis of his work is captured in the title of one of his books, *Why Leaders Can't Lead* (1989). Finally, throughout the 1990s, James M. Kouzes and Barry Z. Posner (1995) analyzed the "leadership challenge." Their focus was to determine how people could keep getting extraordinary things done in organizations.

A content analysis of Hersey and Blanchard, Bennis, Burns, Matusak, and Wheatley results in fourteen critical incidents that we consider to be a leadership paradigm (see Exhibit 2.1). We used this tool to survey twenty-five community college, midlevel administrators from small to very large institutions. There was no attempt to make this study truly scientific, nor were we concerned about gender or ethnicity. The results, however, provide an empirical insight into emergent leadership trends. At least half of the institutions surveyed have gone through major organizational renewal or reorganization within the last five years. Participants in the study range from vice presidents to directors. All of these individuals operate below the senior executive level. Their ages range from late thirties to late fifties; their levels of experience range from five to thirty years. These demographic characteristics appear to be representative of what is occurring in American community colleges on the eve of the millennium.

Community colleges as public sector agencies are not operating in a unified leadership context. To create broader insight, we also surveyed fourteen midlevel managers from a comprehensive regional hospital. The reason for selecting this control group was twofold. First, the organization is going through extensive redevelopment. Second, societal changes are having as much impact on medicine as they are having on education. Our perception was that if the critical incidents of leadership emerge in a similar fashion from both environments, then the recommendations from leadership theory have some utility for managing change. All of the hospital participants are classified as midlevel managers.

Findings

In general there was more similarity than difference among educators in their choices of essential leadership elements. The sample was drawn from midlevel administrators in credit and credit-free programming. The top six essential elements of leadership as defined by credit administrators include admitting and learning from mistakes, breaking down communication barriers, being open to different ways of accomplishing old tasks, listening, and promoting teamwork. For credit-free administrators, the top five elements are honesty, serving as a change agent, promoting teamwork, admitting and learning from mistakes, and listening.

There is sufficient consistency between these midlevel managers in education to draw several viable generalizations. First, leadership with and through people is a theme that permeates this study. Second, an emphasis on teamwork emerges as critical. Finally, the recognition that change brings with it multidimensional challenges results in the need for learning from mistakes.

Is the hospital environment any different? The top five elements reported by midlevel managers include honesty, learning from mistakes, accessibility, emphasizing teamwork, and admitting mistakes. In general, leadership during times of change seems to require initiative and a presentation of self in a truly open, situational mode.

To what extent are midlevel administrators able to implement their personal design for leadership? The top five critical incidents that credit administrators are able to use in their positions include being honest, learning from mistakes, listening, being accessible to constituents, and admitting mistakes. For credit-free administrators the top five are honesty, admitting mistakes, promoting teamwork, learning from mistakes, and taking risks.

One overwhelming insight emerges from these findings. Midlevel community college leaders are dealing with change as it is encountered even though they are not necessarily serving as change agents. They perceive their role as requiring honesty, working with colleagues, and learning from the challenges presented by both internal and external demands.

How does the medical community implement leadership? The top five incidents include honesty, learning from mistakes, promoting teamwork, listening, and admitting mistakes. The congruence reinforces the reliability of the behaviors in managing change in both social settings.

The final dimension of the study was projective. We asked participants in the study to state in two or three sentences their approach to leadership. Their insights are fascinating in that they reinforce the critical perspective designed by Matusak (1997) in her national study on learning to lead from where you are.

Conclusion: You Must Lead

Matusak's (1997) Kellogg study presents a practical blueprint for infusing situational leadership into an organizational context. To bring focus to the qualitative component of our study, we use her five steps along the path to effective leadership. Each step is reinforced by concepts drawn from the participants' open-ended responses.

First Step: Weaving a Shared Vision. Matusak suggests that vision begins with insight, develops intentions, and creates an understanding of a better way of accomplishing critical tasks. A continuing education dean reports, "My notion [of] and approach to leadership is to provide a vision and then nourish the people to help me realize the vision. Facilitation is a key to my approach." Matusak's synthesis reminds us that without the vision and its facilitation, the weaving is impossible.

Second Step: Appreciating a Kaleidoscope of Views. Matusak makes clear that leaders will fail if they continue to view processes or situations through a singular lens of their own specialization, culture, or experience. They must draw on the collective expertise of the organization yet maintain a concern for personal identity. An instructional vice president suggests that leadership requires the generation of "ideas and [to] encourage constituents to develop and present new ideas and strategies in the academic area." The recommendation that none of us individually is as strong as all of us collectively permeates the Kellogg study. The author reminds us that both creativity and trust are hallmarks of environments in which people feel respected, valued, and accepted.

Third Step: Practicing Effective Communication. Matusak defines communication in a very broad context. She assesses effective word choice, nonverbal presentation, listening, and patience in determining actual meaning. Time spent in carefully determining the perspective of the presenter will save significant time in restructuring a misperception or rebuilding a loss of trust.

A critical-care unit manager from the hospital in our study presented a five-step process for the interaction component of leadership:

- On policies that affect everyone, be fair to all—no favorites.
- Provide open, honest communication.
- Answer rumors with facts to stop them.
- Be accessible.
- Role-model professionalism both on and off the job.

Matusak's synthesis of effective communication reinforces the preceding process: "Saying what you believe in an objective, open, honest, nonpersonal way quickly eliminates suspicion and paranoia" (p. 78). It also helps to solidify team initiative.

Fourth Step: Deciding How to Decide. Decision making is essential to all aspects of leadership. The Kellogg Study is insightful in that it suggests that there are a variety of styles for decision making and each of them has a place in the organization of the twenty-first century. Also, the study reveals that all decision making, no matter what model is used, must have as a base a set of moral principles, values, or ethics. A clinical coordinator in the hospital setting synthesizes the decision-making process effectively: "Lead by example, role-modeling, 'walk the talk.' Building a loyal team through flexibility, understanding. Use opportunities to teach from 'wherever you are.'"

The characteristics of decision making presented in the Kellogg Study—open, prompt, caring, and ethical—are well attuned to the changing demands of the coming millennium.

Fifth Step: Creating the Future. Matusak uses this step to assess change management. She presents a rather interesting perspective: "Change has considerable psychological impact on the human mind. *To the fearful,* change is threatening because it means that things may get worse. *To the hopeful,* change is encouraging because things may get better. *To the confident,* change is inspiring because the challenge exists to make things better," (p. 133). To survive into the twenty-first century, it is essential that we collaborate to make things better.

A continuing education dean we surveyed describes the change management process: "Leading in today's dynamic environment requires vision, excellent communication skills, patience, and energy. I believe that my institution must change to continue to thrive; without effective leadership, it will not change." This statement is consistent with the Kellogg position that change management requires deliberate personal and organizational attention.

These five steps provide an accurate blueprint for community college leaders as they prepare to engage the challenges of the millennium. Margaret Wheatley's (1992) work on leadership provides us with two helpful perspectives for the engagement. Her assessment suggests that we reach out to and work with leaders who are committed to creating shared meaning. These people give focus and direction to individuals' search for meaning and help make the organization's mission purposeful. They are cherished. She also extracts from the scientific context the importance of field and ground. "Leadership is *always* dependent on the context, but the context is established by the *relationships* we value. We cannot hope to influence any situation without respect for the complex network of people who contribute to our organizations" (p. 144).

Will community colleges meet the challenges of the millennium? Our research leaves us optimistic. We are hopeful; we are confident. The behavior revealed in the study of midlevel community college educational leaders reinforces the importance of leading from where you are and suggests that we are likely to be successful.

References

Bennis, W. *Why Leaders Can't Lead: The Unconscious Conspiracy Continues.* San Francisco: Jossey-Bass, 1989.

Burns, J. M. *Leadership.* New York: HarperCollins, 1978.

Hersey, P., and Blanchard, K. *Management of Organizational Behavior: Utilizing Human Resources.* (4th ed.) Englewood Cliffs, N.J.: Prentice Hall, 1982.

Kline, P., and Saunders, B. *Ten Steps to a Learning Organization.* (2nd ed.) Arlington, Va.: Great Ocean, 1998.

Kouzes, J. M., and Posner, B. Z. *The Leadership Challenge: How to Keep Getting Extraordinary Things Done in Organizations.* (2nd ed.) San Francisco: Jossey-Bass, 1995.

Matusak, L. R. *Finding Your Voice: Learning to Lead . . . Anywhere You Want to Make a Difference.* San Francisco: Jossey-Bass, 1997.

Norris, D. M. "Fusion and the Knowledge Age." *NACUBO Business Officer,* 1998, *31* (7), 36.

Wheatley, M. J. *Leadership and the New Science: Learning About Organizations from an Orderly Universe.* San Francisco: Berrett-Koehler, 1992.

ROBIN L. SPAID is associate dean, Continuing Education and Economic Development, Hagerstown Junior College, Maryland.

MICHAEL H. PARSONS is dean of instruction, Hagerstown Junior College, Maryland.

*Managers in a large multicollege district voluntarily created the
Administrative Leadership Institute, a systematic approach to midlevel
management development.*

The Practitioner's Guide to Midlevel Management Development

Mary S. Spangler

A key element in the continued success of community colleges and in their
ability to adapt to and change with the current environment lies in the capacity of those who manage and lead to perform effectively. Although professional development activities and programs are widely available, in at least
one large multicollege district there was a significant absence of systemic
midlevel management training. This chapter describes how the Administrative Leadership Institute (ALI), one specific response to the situation, was
conceptualized, developed, and implemented over a three-year period. The
discussion begins with the rationale for this approach to professional development, describes the stages in ALI's development, outlines the program
model and contents, provides outcome information on the first year of its
implementation, and concludes by recommending development strategies
for other organizations.

The Need for Systemic Leadership Training

Based on the recognition of a need for midlevel management development, the
ALI program is grounded in several basic assumptions. These include that
administrators and managers value collegiality, are responsible for demonstrating leadership, have the requisite skills as individuals but can benefit the
organization and themselves through a group-oriented program, and recognize
the importance for the organization to prepare new leaders continuously.

In California, professional development funds are provided to districts by
the state, but the way funds are expended is determined by the receiving institutions. Generally the funds are used by individuals to attend conferences and

workshops pertaining to their particular interest or discipline, area of expertise, or self-acknowledged need for specialized training. Kim (1993) states that "organizations ultimately learn via their individual members" (p. 37) through a transfer of the learning that occurs between the individual and the organization. Training by and within an organization of a cohort of individuals already in midlevel positions or interested in moving into such positions remains unaddressed. Training programs like the National Chair Academy and the Franklin Covey Institute are excluded from this discussion because they are generally attended by individuals rather than by a cohort from a community college district or system. Consequently, the opportunity to create a critical mass within the organization to enable it to be a learning organization (Senge, 1990) is generally untapped or lost.

Another reality readily observed within larger community college districts and documented in the practitioners' literature is that those moving into midlevel management positions, and managers and administrators moving to higher positions, generally do so without formal training to assist them. Thus the management and delivery of the organization's services, the expansion of management skills and knowledge base, and the ability to recognize and respond to external demands and challenges can be affected to the detriment of the organization.

Rapid and radical change threatens the vitality of many community colleges, yet the role of academic leaders is to manage the transformation process effectively (Carter and Alfred, 1996; Lorenzo and Zajac, 1996). Covey (1992) states, "Training and development programs should evolve naturally from the [organization's] vision, mission, and principles. Programs should attempt to empower people to soar, to sail, to step forward bravely into the unknown" (p. 72).

Against the background of change and the stresses and demands attending this reality, leaders at all levels are concerned with how to survive and succeed, how to develop a sense of the future, and how to instill skills that will shape leaders at the departmental or organizational level (McAdams, 1996). Carter and Alfred (1996) note that theory and past practice do not provide guidance in this uncharted territory but trial and error abound. Gmelch and Houchen (1994) use the term *amateur administration* to identify faculty moving into the administrative ranks as department chair. Seagren and Dockery (1996) indicate that training is necessary for the successful management of decline and competition, yet higher education institutions are "among the few organizations that do not provide training for middle management" (p. 33). The Los Angeles Community College District (LACCD) is an organization that reflects these conditions.

The literature identifies the skills necessary for leadership and the roles and accompanying responsibilities that administrators should perform. It also addresses the challenges to sustaining the transformation process. Formal education in these areas has been assumed primarily by university programs and by separate conferences, symposia, and workshops. Yet constraints imposed by the institution and by outside agencies complicate the confluence of responsibility and time urgency and, often significantly, threaten administrators' abilities to function, adapt, and transform when and where necessary. Diamond (1996) addresses the complex tasks facing today's unprepared managers: "The time has passed when this crucial position [of department chairperson or higher-level administrator] can be a pre-retirement stopover or an assignment that faculty members take turns at filling simply because 'someone has to do it'" (p. B2).

Establishing the Administrative Leadership Institute

The LACCD is one of seventy-one community college districts in California and the largest in the nation. It is a public, nine-college district with a service area of 882 square miles. With approximately 100,000 students of the 1.5 million enrolled annually in community colleges throughout the state, the LACCD is diverse in its ethnic makeup: 42 percent of its student population is Hispanic, 23 percent is white, 18 percent is African American, 15 percent is Asian, and 2 percent is other. Personnel include 123 administrators and managers, 1,498 full-time and 2,048 part-time faculty, and 5,916 staff.

The size and complexity of the organization inevitably mean that simultaneously there are multiple positions either vacant or filled on an acting basis. This situation undermines the organization's stability. In recent years the Accrediting Commission of the Western Association of Schools and Colleges has consistently noted this condition as a negative factor in the LACCD's operation and recommended filling such positions. A high turnover rate, however, combined with inadequate formal training and an often-inexperienced candidate pool, continues to undermine the district's ability to address adequately its fiscal and operational responsibilities. At least among senior administrators, however, there has been a relatively recent attempt to counteract the problem with the proactive, internal ALI program.

Stages in ALI's Development

The idea for a systemic approach to leadership development originated in June 1995 with a group of twenty senior administrators from the nine colleges and the district office who selected as a primary educational goal the development of an in-district training program. They recognized the need for a coherent, focused way to upgrade and expand the management skills of administrators while preparing potential administrators. The following major stages and activities trace the program's evolution.

Development of Preliminary Draft. This first stage lasted from September 1995 to February 1996. After the resolution to develop the concept was approved by the chancellor, nine committed volunteer administrators assembled from academic affairs, student services, and administrative services formed the ALI advisory board. They developed programmatic assumptions, created a mission statement, articulated the benefits, and identified possible workshop topics.

Presentation for Cabinet Approval. In April 1996 a preliminary draft was presented to the cabinet for review and discussion. Program components were approved, and funding sources and needs were considered, but no action was taken. Funding was the most difficult challenge to overcome. The advisory board members could not implement, manage, and conduct the programs without significant auxiliary support; consequently, a substantial commitment to fund the program was essential for it to be implemented.

Development of Program Model. From May 1996 to September 1996, the advisory board met monthly to develop themes for workshops, consider delivery strategies, refine funding needs, develop a preliminary budget, and create a draft packet of materials for distribution.

The initial budget request included the costs to establish the project, a budget projection for an eighteen-month program of workshops and program evaluation at the end of one full year of operation, and the cost of establishing an internship program to begin in the second semester of the second year. Because funding for the second year has been significantly reduced, this internship component was redesigned to be less ambitious.

Planning. This stage lasted from October 1996 to January 1997. Despite a convoluted, lengthy development and approval process, the advisory board secured $15,000 from the chancellor's discretionary funds as "seed" money and initiated the program in the spring of 1997. These funds represented 12 percent of the final budget. The board developed the final calendar of activities and recruitment strategies; created an information brochure, application, and strategies for recruiting; finalized the program for the first colloquium; and arranged locations for the workshops. They also were successful later in securing full funding from the chancellor's discretionary budget for one year. The final budget of $115,000 was 8 percent less than the original request. During the program's initial year, the district office used its own funds to cover all but $65,000 of two contracts. Other costs were absorbed by the colleges' operating budgets or by the registration fees assessed to participants.

The final approved 1997-98 budget reflected the expectation that office space and furnishings would be provided by the district and that the program would not be charged for utilities, maintenance, or supplies.

Implementation. From January 1997 to May 1997, the advisory board developed a districtwide communication process, trained the area representatives to recruit at each college, received applications, and notified applicants of their status. The recruitment activities resulted in 240 individuals completing an application.

An outside consultant was selected to implement the approved program. Competitive bidding was undertaken and the contract was awarded to Company of Experts, a professional development consulting firm specializing in community college clients. The one-year contract was to manage registration, develop workshop materials and workshop presentations as approved by the advisory board, and schedule and conduct the yearlong workshops.

Regular programming began in September 1997 and continues as of this writing. Projected financial shortfalls within the district during spring 1998 limited the district's willingness to provide continuing financial support. Outside funding was sought unsuccessfully; the 1998-99 program has been reduced in scope to rely on internal resources and in-house facilitators. The district's staff development committee is cosponsoring the program and providing $6,500 in exchange for opening access to the monthly workshops to all interested employees. Thus, during the second year, registration fees to participants will increase from $10 to $12.

The ALI Program Model

The ALI is a systemic approach to middle management training designed to be meaningful in content, feasible to implement, and attractive to employees. In developing the program, the advisory board wrote a mission statement and goals, selected program segments, recruited participants, and developed informational materials.

Mission and Goals. ALI's mission is to provide a supportive environment characterized by respect, collegiality, and trust among and for its managers. Through a structured series of colloquia, presentations, and workshops, current and potential managers can expand their skills and strengthen their effectiveness as educational leaders (Administrative Leadership Institute, 1996).

To achieve its mission, the advisory board identified three key goals: to expose participants to various models of administration, to create a resource for current administrators and a learning environment for potential managers, and to provide professional opportunities for pleasurable and productive learning. Additional objectives include improving communication among the administrative staff, providing information for long-range planning, strengthening leadership morale, and utilizing human resources more effectively within the district.

Program Segments. The eighteen-month program consists of three semester-long segments of workshops framed by three themes: administrative concepts (for example, team building, managing good employees, and risk taking), survival skills (for example, interview techniques, stress management, and establishing priorities), and applied knowledge (for example, employee supervision, budget preparation, hiring processes, and contractual issues). The content is based on a survey response to potential topics. Sessions combine a variety of strategies and materials to encourage group interaction, problem solving, and application to daily tasks.

In its first year, to accommodate schedules and maximize participation, ALI offered workshops on different themes over an eight-month period. Each workshop was repeated on two consecutive days during the month so that a total of sixteen sessions were offered. The workshops covered the following topics: leading, problem solving, and managing change; building teams; communicating;

developing organizational climate and motivating; managing and supervising; managing time, health, and wellness; and making decisions.

In its second year, participants attend a single monthly workshop designed and facilitated in-house. Each moderator is responsible for developing a program in the area of applied knowledge. The advisory board acts as a resource to coordinate the agenda and to recruit district personnel who are recognized experts on the topics.

In addition to the workshops, a fall and a spring colloquium and a three-day workshop on principle-centered leadership are offered. The spring 1998 colloquium was hosted by the University of California Los Angeles's Graduate School of Education and Information Sciences, based on their awareness of ALI's success. The positive response to the first program has secured a commitment to hold another joint colloquium in May 1999.

Qualified participants may also apply for a fourth-semester intern project. An applicant must have accumulated at least twelve of a possible eighteen points from attending the monthly activities; each ALI activity counts as one point. The advisory board is currently reviewing and evaluating the applicants' requests in order to match the interns with the locations and mentors selected.

Recruitment. Although the ALI was first conceptualized as being for current administrators, participation is open to all regular, full-time employees who are leaders, managers, or both. The positive response emphasizes the need for such a program and that a systemic approach to professional development is appropriate.

The advisory board considered several strategies to recruit ALI participants and decided to invite one certified administrator and one classified manager from each location to recruit as a team for membership at their locations. A recruitment training session includes familiarizing the team with ALI's formation, its goals and benefits, and its strategies on approaching current and potential midlevel managers.

As area representatives, the team members also serve as liaisons to the advisory board. This approach helps broaden involvement and provides an opportunity for leadership experience. In addition, the team knows best the culture of their college and therefore is better able to approach potential applicants and present the materials effectively. The team also functions to share the workload by disseminating ALI newsletters and announcements on their campuses.

Informational Materials. The advisory board identified Administrative Leadership Institute as the name for the program to emphasize the primary goal of attracting, preparing, and strengthening administrators and managers. A logo, masthead, and stationery layout were developed so that ongoing communications would be identified with the program. A recruitment brochure and application include ALI's mission statement, goals, benefits, thematic workshops, and enrollment information. A newsletter to maintain communication and encourage networking was created and published monthly by the consultant. In the second year, the advisory board assumed this task. The consultant also created and assembled into notebooks the materials developed for the workshops.

Evaluation Measures. The advisory board assigned the collection of data to the consultant and the analysis of data to an institutional researcher. For each activity, the consultant asked open-ended questions in the areas of content, process, and environment and rated the responses on a ten-point scale. The results are reported in the monthly newsletter. The highest marks of the series were recorded in May 1998 for the topic "making decisions and delegating," with 9.4 reported for content, 9.3 for process, and 8.9 for environment. The advisory board also distributed its own assessment tool, a questionnaire of five items on a five-point scale. The questions ask to what degree information is useful in developing leadership skills, how it will be applied in the person's current position, whether it is useful in furthering career goals, whether the workshop will be recommended to colleagues, and if it meets the person's expectations in terms of ALI's goals. An analysis of the survey data collected from ALI activities from March 1997 to March 1998 reveals a range of scores from 4.04 to 4.83, with an overall evaluation of all activities at 4.31.

These high marks, in addition to requests for the workshops to continue and inquiries about new enrollments, supported the decision to continue ALI for another year, despite limited funds, with the modifications previously described. Adequate financial support would improve the assessment of the information that has been regularly collected.

Recommendations and Findings

The experience of developing a concept into a reality proves that it is worth doing. In the process, friends are made, skills are learned, people are influenced, and attitudes mature. In the absence of a directive to create and maintain such an ambitious program, however, individuals may be frustrated in carrying a project from inception to expression. Other attempts to initiate a leadership program may well require a commitment to fund the activities before individuals are willing to spend time beyond their regular responsibilities working together to develop a concept. To increase the likelihood that the elusive opportunity to create critical mass and effect change will succeed, several recommendations are offered:

Assemble a team of individuals with a high degree of responsibility and a willingness to accept additional work and to share and learn together.

Meet on a regular basis, differentiate and assign tasks, and set goals and deadlines while keeping the meetings fun and informal.

Hold the needs of the organization clearly in mind while keeping the planning group small and focused on the tasks.

In the early stages especially, ensure that upper-level decision makers are fully informed of the planning group's progress, needs, and expectations.

Once the program is approved and funding is identified, select a contact person to facilitate and manage its implementation, handle the distribution of information and registration materials, and conduct an assessment and evaluation of its effectiveness.

Provide a communication vehicle for the participants, inform supervisors of participants' contributions to management-related activities, share credit with all involved, and distribute evaluative data widely.

Concluding Thoughts

An apparently small initial effort to meet a real need has unintentionally become part of the catalyst for change embarked on within the LACCD. This agent for change is producing discernible outcomes in the areas of promotion, goodwill, and skill development. Had the task of creating the project been assigned to an individual administrator, it is likely that the ALI would still be a fleeting thought, a good idea not enacted. Instead, it is a dynamic change agent sustained by teamwork, fun, and commitment. Despite the lack of stable funding, those who have participated in its formation and continuing development have experienced firsthand the challenges and rewards of personal leadership.

References

Administrative Leadership Institute. *Administrative Leadership Institute Mission Statement.* Los Angeles: Administrative Leadership Institute, Dec. 1996.

Carter, P., and Alfred, R. L. "Transforming Community Colleges to Compete for the Future: Why the Tried and True Is Now Old Hat." *Academic Leadership,* 1996, *3* (3), 3–7.

Covey, S. *Principle-Centered Leadership.* New York: Simon & Schuster, 1992.

Diamond, R. M. "What It Takes to Lead a Department." *Chronicle of Higher Education,* Jan. 5, 1996, pp. B1–B2.

Gmelch, W. H., and Houchen, B. C. "The Balancing Act of Community College Chairs." *Academic Leadership,* 1994, *2* (1), 5–11.

Kim, D. "The Link Between Individual and Organization Learning." *Sloan Management Review,* 1993, *35* (1), 37–50.

Lorenzo, A. L., and Zajac, C. S. "A Penny for Your Thoughts: Improving Organizations Through Change." *Academic Leadership,* 1996, *3* (3), 15–19.

McAdams, R. P. "Revitalizing the Department Chair: Ten Recommendations to Make the Role More Attractive, Powerful, and Effective." *AAHE Bulletin,* 1996, *49* (6), 10–13.

Seagren, A. T., and Dockery, M. S. "Academic Leadership: Past, Present, and Future." *Academic Leadership,* 1996, *3* (3), 33–34.

Senge, P. M. *The Fifth Discipline: The Art and Practice of the Learning Organization.* New York: Doubleday, 1990.

MARY S. SPANGLER is president of Los Angeles City College and founder and chair of the Administrative Leadership Institute's advisory board.

Workplace socialization theory is a useful framework for understanding the experiences of new department chairs and for meeting their professional development needs.

A Statewide Survey of New Department Chairs: Their Experiences and Needs in Learning Their Roles

Albert B. Smith, Gloria A. Stewart

The academic administrator is vital to institutions of higher education that are redirecting their efforts, moving forward toward new organizational forms, and creating climates conducive to cooperation and collaboration among divergent constituencies (Creswell and others, 1990; Seagren, Creswell, and Wheeler, 1993). Yet many of those who assume the role of department or division chair in community colleges are not prepared for what is in store—a multiplicity of demands, long hours, and a change in perspective (Seagren and others, 1994). Many find themselves "learning the ropes" as they go along—thus making an inherently stressful role even more so (Tucker, 1993).

A variety of factors can hinder or facilitate the new chair's transition into her or his role. Among these factors are the skills and knowledge brought from previous faculty roles, the impact of unexpected elements of the new job, and how the individual goes about learning the demands of tasks, roles, and interpersonal relationships. If indeed most new two-year-college chairs learn how to function in their roles through informal and discovery learning (that is, by consulting colleagues or by doing, watching, and reading), then it appears that institutions should facilitate and support these activities in addition to providing formal training and development opportunities. When tasks, roles, and interpersonal relationships assigned to an administrative position are improperly discharged, the effectiveness of the organization as a whole is impaired. Developing a deeper understanding of the role-transitioning process of new department chairs will assist administrators and faculty in evaluating the efficacy of current practices as well as in equipping newly appointed chairs for success.

Nature of the Study

The purposes of this study were to profile department and division chairpersons appointed in the 1995–96 academic year at community colleges in Texas and to gain an understanding of the role-transitioning process based on the perceptions of these individuals. Eventually this research will be used to suggest methods and processes that might better facilitate role transitioning of first-time department and division chairs in community colleges.

Conceptual Framework. The theoretical framework guiding this study is the process of socialization within organizations. The terms *socialization, workplace socialization, role socialization,* and *role transitioning* are used synonymously. Socialization is a series of stages that an individual undergoes in making the transition from one position to another within an organization, as well as when making the transition into an organization from the outside (Getzels, 1958; Morton, 1993; Rusaw, 1995). Role socialization is the process of learning expected values, attitudes, and behaviors associated with a position in an organization as well as learning the tasks and interpersonal relationships associated with the position.

Figure 4.1 illustrates the four stages of socialization within organizations—anticipation, encounter, adaptation, and withdrawal. This cycle may be repeated many times throughout an individual's career as she or he switches jobs within an organization, moves to other organizations, or leaves the work force.

Because the focus of this study is workplace socialization from the perspective of learning in the workplace, only Stages 1 through Stage 3 are pertinent. The *anticipation* stage is antecedent to organizational entry or appointment to the position of department or division chair and includes what the newcomer brings to the new position—skills and knowledge gained through formal, informal, and discovery learning efforts and work experience. When the newly appointed chairperson assumes the position, the second stage, *encounter,* begins. The third stage, *adaptation,* also known as *assimilation,* relates to the signals received from the organization and from the individual that a successful role transition has been made. What organizations do (such as formalizing orienta-

Figure 4.1. Generic Representation of the Theoretical Stages of Workplace Socialization

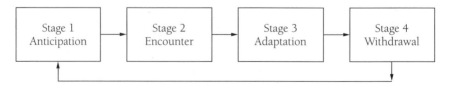

Source: Adapted from Nelson, 1990, and Morton, 1993.

tion activities or taking the posture of learn as you go) and what individuals do (such as learning acceptable behaviors by observing role models) to promote role transitioning become the building blocks of successful adaptation (organizational and incumbent signals) to a new role (Katz and Kahn, 1966; Louis, 1990; Schein, 1992).

Research Question. This study explored how chairs learned their roles—what skills and knowledge they brought to the position (*anticipation*), how they went about learning their role (*encounter*), and how they assimilated into the role (*adaptation*). The primary research question was, What is the profile of new department or division chairpersons in two-year institutions of higher education in Texas with respect to demographic characteristics and role transition variables?

Methodology. This study used survey research techniques to investigate how new chairs went about learning the tasks, roles, and interpersonal demands of their position. Eleven survey items addressed the chair's stages of role transitioning—anticipation, encounter, and adaptation. Another twelve questions sought information regarding the respondent's institution, department, and personal data. Item-response scales for the first eleven questions were constructed using five-point Likert continuums, with possible response choices ranging from "strongly agree" (5) to "strongly disagree" (1).

Based on information provided by representatives at 163 higher education institutions in Texas contacted in fall 1996, a total of 193 new chairs appointed in 1995–96 were identified. Of these chairs, 99 (or 51 percent) worked in community colleges. Of the 99 new community college chairs, 59 (or 60 percent) responded to the twenty-three-item questionnaire in fall 1997. Data from this group of 59 responding community college chairs form the basis of this chapter.

Major Findings Related to Background and Preparation Characteristics

New community college (CC) chairs in Texas were predominately White (71 percent), with the next largest group (10 percent) being Black. With respect to age, the largest group (44 percent) fell in the 50 to 59 range, with the next largest group (41 percent) falling in the 40 to 49 range. Thirty-nine percent of the new chairs were female, showing that the new chairs reflect the general male-female composition of community college faculties nationally. The greatest number of new chairs reported holding a master's degree (59 percent), followed by 20 percent holding a doctorate. Few new chairs (only 15 percent) reported being nontenured, with most (85 percent) being tenured.

These findings are not surprising, except that one might have expected a larger percentage of Hispanics among the new chairs given the increasing percentage of Hispanic faculty and students in Texas community colleges. One additional training area for new or established chairs might be in the state's higher education doctoral programs, because only 20 percent of the new community college chairs in this study held a doctoral degree.

One other interesting finding is that only 59 percent of the chairs lasted more than two years in their position after their 1995–96 appointment. It was found that 12 percent (seven) of the fifty-nine chairs lasted only one year and 29 percent (seventeen) lasted only two years. This finding alone suggests that there may be a need for more effective education and training of chairs, particularly if colleges are concerned about consistent leadership at this most important level of administration.

With respect to whether ongoing training was required, encouraged, or offered on a purely voluntary basis, we found that only in six cases (10 percent) did the chairs report that formal training was an ongoing requirement in their colleges. Fifty-two percent, or thirty-one, of the chairs indicated that formal, ongoing training was encouraged, and 37 percent, or twenty-two, chairs noted that training was only on a voluntary basis.

Regarding length of appointment, we were surprised to find that forty-six of the fifty-nine new chairs (78 percent) reported that their appointments were ongoing with no term limits. We had expected to find more definite term limits that would provide deans with periodic opportunities to evaluate a chair's work after three to six years. Contrary to current literature, the department chairs do not appear to be in short-term appointments.

For the most part, new CC chairs in Texas are classified as faculty with part-time administrative duties. Fifty-four percent (thirty-two of the fifty-nine new chairs) described themselves as part-time administrators. Some questions could be raised here. Would it be better to have CC chairs as administrators with part-time faculty duties? Would it lead to more effective leadership in community college departments and divisions if chairs saw themselves as administrators with important leadership responsibilities rather than as being primarily faculty members?

Finally, we found that the fifty-nine new CC chairs were fairly evenly distributed across disciplines: 34 percent were academic, 44 percent were vocational-technical, and 22 percent were academic-technical. We did not study these three groups separately, although it may be interesting to do so in the future.

Given the importance of this position in two-year colleges and given most new chairs' apparent lack of knowledge of administration, policies need to be established that require initial as well as ongoing formal training and development of new CC chairs. The need for more formal training, something that many CC deans and presidents currently have, was evident in many of the comments received from chairs after they had completed their questionnaires, such as the following:

Formal training should be provided by the institution. There are administrative requirements, policies, rules, business procedures, and so on, including budgeting issues that are generic to the institution. Receiving training in these areas and receiving an operations manual will assist tremendously in getting acclimated to the position.

Basically, I was thrown into the job with practically no training. If it had not been for relationships formed while I was a faculty member, I would have been totally lost. Thank goodness I don't mind asking hundreds of questions. I got most of my answers from administrative assistants. I would never want to go through what I went through. I think other department heads look at it as a form of hazing—I did it, so you have to do it too.

These two comments are typical of those received from many chairs who had no prior administrative experience. There appears to be a genuine interest in the process of role transitioning among new CC chairs. Fifty-four percent of the 59 chairs provided comments regarding their experiences, and 88 percent requested a copy of the survey results.

Perhaps one of the most revealing questions asked in the survey questionnaire was, How long did it take you to feel comfortable in your position as a chair? The majority of the new chairs (thirty-four, or 58 percent), reported that it took them six months to feel comfortable in their new positions. Although this is good news, such a comfort level could probably be achieved in a shorter period if formal training were required of chairs for a year prior to their new appointments. The fact that ten of the fifty-nine new chairs reported not feeling comfortable in their new role until two or more years after their appointment is a troubling statistic. This finding led to further exploration of the questions, How do new CC chairs learn their roles? and Can a model showing how chairs learn their roles be developed for use in administrative development programs for prospective or new chairs?

Major Findings Related to New Chair Experiences and Needs

The rest of this chapter relates what the fifty-nine chairs had to say about their transitions into the chair role. In this part of the study, the chairs were asked to respond to fifty-nine questions.

Anticipation (Stage 1). CC chairs reported having very little formal learning to prepare themselves for the position. Taking courses for credit, attending in-house workshops, or going to outside workshops on administrative issues were activities used only to a slight extent by a majority of the respondents (thirty-six, or 61 percent). By far the most frequently mentioned ways in which these new CC chairs learned their roles was through informal, self-guided activities or from prior work experiences. To a great extent these new chairs reported learning their roles informally from previous administrative duties, by serving on committees, by reading books and journals, and by observing role models. They reported that their previous task demands, role demands, and interpersonal relationships greatly helped them to prepare for the demands of the chair position.

Encounter (Stage 2). Chairs strongly agreed that their orientation was informal and individualized within the ongoing work of their unit. They also tended to disagree strongly that their orientation was sequential, orderly, or provided by their predecessor. They did, however, tend to perceive the established members of their units as accepting rather than challenging their abilities to do the job.

The new chairs were asked what unexpected events or surprises they found in the chair's role. The greatest shock or unexpected activity reported was the amount of paperwork involved. Twenty-seven (46 percent) of the fifty-nine chairs gave this area either the highest rating (5) or the second highest rating (4). The other two shocking areas were found to be the large amount of time that administrative duties consumed and becoming a public figure with constant interruptions.

With respect to their organizational cultures, the new chairs tended to feel that once they were in their positions, risk taking was not greatly encouraged, and equipment and material resources they needed to learn their jobs were not ample or easily accessible. On a positive note, they tended to agree that knowledge and skills were generously shared among members of the college. The organizational milieu in community colleges appears to be a mixed bag when it comes to being supportive of chairs learning their roles.

On another positive note, the new CC chairs tended to be somewhat satisfied with the support, on-the-job learning experiences, positive experiences, and performance feedback they received in their new positions. However, on only one out of four of these items did the chairs' mean responses fall in the "strongly agree" range. Why more new chairs are not responding that their first-year and second-year experiences are very satisfying should be a major concern of their supervisors.

Earlier in this chapter it was noted that new CC chairs in Texas reported that their learning of the chair's role prior to assuming the chairmanship was more likely to be informal and self-guided rather than formal. We found that such patterns of informal and discovery or self-directed learning were also the more frequently used methods of learning by chairs once they were on the job. The most often reported method of learning on the job was "by doing" followed by "consulting with a superior in the organization." Other popular learning strategies appear to be of an informal or discovery nature as well, such as talking to peer experts inside the institution or reading books, magazines, and manuals.

Clearly the least-used on-the-job method of learning by new CC chairs is the formal learning strategy of taking a university-sponsored course for credit. Thirty-nine of the new CC chairs reported having never taken a university course after their appointment to learn their new roles, and another eleven individuals said they rarely have taken a credit course at a university to learn more about their roles. This last finding perhaps suggests a new challenge for community college educators located near or in university higher education programs. Community college education programs need to find new ways to serve this important group of leaders.

With respect to their views on interpersonal relationships, the new Texas chairs tended to show a good deal of confidence. They were in fairly strong agreement that they knew who could give them answers, who was interested in helping them, whom they could go to when they wanted to get something done (that is, whom they could select as confidantes), who were their most respected colleagues, and who had the power to get things done (that is, who were the key upper-level administrators). These particular findings may point to one of the first qualities a dean looks for in selecting a new chair, that is, the ability to get along with a wide range of people. This may be an area in which new chairs need the least amount of preparation for their new roles.

Adaptation (Stage 3). How are the new CC chairs adapting to their roles in Texas community colleges? If we had found that they were adapting very well to their new surroundings, then there would be very little need to continue this research. This was not the case.

The chairs' perceptions of their adaptation activities proved to be a mixed bag. In terms of organizational signals, there was a fairly strong tendency for the fifty-nine chairs to strongly agree that they had received a favorable performance evaluation. Twenty-two new chairs (37 percent) circled the highest possible response (5) related to their performance evaluations, and another 26 (44 percent) circled 4, indicating that they too agreed that they had received a favorable performance evaluation. Eleven chairs, however, circled a neutral response for this item, indicating that they were having difficulty deciding whether they had had a favorable performance evaluation. These eleven individuals could probably have had a more positive evaluation if they had been better prepared for their roles by their institutions.

The two-year-college chairs we surveyed tended not to see themselves as insiders. Also, a majority of them reported not receiving an award or other recognition for their work. These may be two reasons why twenty-four of the surveyed chairs (41 percent) did not stay in their new positions more than two years.

Another negative finding of this research was that 36 percent, or twenty-one, of the CC chairs agreed or strongly agreed that they often thought about returning to a faculty position. Community colleges need chairs who are excited about leading their departments for at least three to five years. It is not a healthy situation for community colleges to have a majority of their new chairs saying that they are either essentially neutral or that they would not recommend assuming a chair position to others. In this study, thirty-seven (63 percent) of the fifty-nine new chairs responded either that they were neutral (seventeen), that they disagreed (thirteen), or that they strongly disagreed (seven) that they would recommend that others assume a chair position.

Summary

This chapter contains the partial findings of a research study of the experiences and possible needs of new community college department chairs in Texas. The study profiles fifty-nine new chairs with respect to selected background and role transition variables. These research findings clearly seem to point to the need for more formal training of prospective or new community college chairs in Texas as well as in other states. To the extent that community colleges in other states find similar leadership needs expressed by their new and current chairs, these colleges should develop preservice and inservice department chair education programs. For community colleges to remain strong, each two-year college in this country should establish a department chair leadership program for prospective and new department chairs. These programs could be offered on campus, through partnerships with other two-year colleges, or through cooperative programs with nearby university community college leadership programs.

References

Creswell, J. W., Wheeler, D. W., Seagren, A. T., Egly, N. J., and Beyer, K. D. *The Academic Chairperson's Handbook.* Lincoln: University of Nebraska Press, 1990.

Getzels, J. W. "Administration as a Social Process." In A. W. Halpin (ed.), *Administrative Theory in Education.* Chicago: Midwest Administration Center, 1958.

Katz, D., and Kahn, R. L. *The Social Psychology of Organizations.* (2nd ed.) New York: Wiley, 1966.

Louis, M. R. "Acculturation in the Workplace: Newcomers as Lay Ethnographers." In B. Schneider (ed.), *Organization Climate and Culture.* San Francisco: Jossey-Bass, 1990.

Morton, S. T. "Socialization-Related Learning, Job Satisfaction, and Commitment for New Employees in a Federal Agency." Unpublished doctoral dissertation, Virginia Polytechnic Institute and State University, 1993.

Nelson, D. L. "Adjusting to a New Organization: Easing the Transition from Outsider to Insider." *Prevention in Human Services,* 1990, 8 (1), 61–86.

Rusaw, A. C. "Learning by Association: Professional Associations as Learning Agents." *Human Resource Development Quarterly,* 1995, 6 (2), 215–226.

Schein, E. H. *Organizational Culture and Leadership.* (2nd ed.) San Francisco: Jossey-Bass, 1992.

Seagren, A. T., Creswell, J. W., and Wheeler, D. W. *The Department Chair: New Roles, Responsibilities, and Challenges.* ASHE-ERIC Higher Education Report no. 1. Washington, D.C.: School of Education and Human Development, George Washington University, 1993.

Seagren, A. T., Wheeler, D. W., Creswell, J. W., Miller, M. T., and VanHorn-Grassmeyer, K. *Academic Leadership in Community Colleges.* Lincoln: University of Nebraska Press, 1994.

Tucker, A. *Chairing the Academic Department: Leadership Among Peers.* Phoenix: Oryx Press, 1993.

ALBERT B. SMITH *is coordinator of the higher education program and professor at Texas Tech University, Lubbock.*

GLORIA A. STEWART *is director of institutional research at the University of Houston–Downtown and a doctoral student in the higher education program at Texas Tech University, Lubbock.*

*In conversations with six community college presidents, issue editor
Rosemary Gillett-Karam asks about the definitions, roles, essential
skills, and accomplishments of midlevel managers at their respective
institutions.*

College Presidents Examine
Midlevel Management in the
Community College

*Rosemary Gillett-Karam with Donald W. Cameron,
Robert C. Messina, Jr., Stephen K. Mittelstet, Anne E.
Mulder, Abel B. Sykes, Jr., Jerry Sue Thornton*

Midlevel management positions at community colleges tend to be complex and
demanding jobs. For this reason, surveys and other quantitative methodologies may be inadequate tools for gaining a deep understanding of the responsibilities, conflicts, and outcomes these positions entail. Therefore, in an effort
to gain a comprehensive view of the role of the department chair (also known
as division chair or academic dean, among other titles), six current and past
college presidents were interviewed about their perceptions of these individuals at their institutions.

The individuals included in these conversations were

Donald W. Cameron, president, Guilford Technical Community College, NC
Robert C. Messina, Jr., president, Burlington County College, NJ
Stephen K. Mittelstet, president, Richland College, TX
Anne E. Mulder, past president, Lake Michigan College, MI
Abel B. Sykes, Jr., president, Lansing Community College, MI
Jerry Sue Thornton, president, Cuyahoga Community College District, OH

The Interviews

Each president responded to six questions that probed the way their institution defines the role of the chair, the organizational place of these individuals,

the need for these midlevel managers (given the trend in business and industry to eliminate many of these positions), the problems encountered and successes achieved by these individuals, and the qualities embodied by those chairs who handle their positions gracefully.

The six institutions represent a range of sizes, emphases, and locations among community colleges. It is not surprising, therefore, to find that the responses to the questions varied from institution to institution. However, several themes emerged across all interviews. Of primary importance is the conviction of the presidents that, for the present, these positions are essential to smooth operation of the colleges. However, there is no consensus about the extent to which this role will exist in the community college of the twenty-first century. Second, there is recognition that this role is, by definition, subject to significant conflict, because it serves as the interface between faculty and administrative demands. Third, the presidents agree that the most essential trait for success in this position is superior communication skills.

Following is a synopsis of the responses to each of the questions, along with some direct quotations from the conversations with the presidents.

QUESTION 1. *How do you define the position of chair at your college?*

Only two of the presidents interviewed referred to midlevel managers of the academic and vocational areas of their institutions as chairs; the remaining presidents and their institutions called their midlevel managers deans. The one-time chair position is called division dean or academic dean, usually to differentiate this position from a faculty position.

CAMERON: The department chair position meshes administration, student services, administrative services, staff, and instructional areas to ensure quality at Guilford Technical College. To function effectively as a department chair, an individual must possess excellent leadership, management, facilitation, mediation, communication, planning and organizational, evaluation, instruction, public and student relations, and supervision skills. The chair's position and duties are so broad and comprehensive that all known skills must be utilized by the successful department chair. The chair must communicate effectively to the faculty, staff, and students the policies and goals of the college. The chairs have responsibility to see that these policies are adhered to uniformly and that the goals of the college are met.

MITTELSTET: Division deans represent midlevel management at Richland College; they are responsible for academic units such as humanities, sciences and math, communications, world languages, business as well as instruction (adjunct faculty dean), and human and academic development. They are liaisons to the community involved in public school articulation, tech-prep, and recruitment of students. They play a role in keeping current in new program exploration. They allow us to be successful in keeping this place open on a day-to-day basis. We count on these leaders for program review, summary information, narrative and context data, [and] personnel recommendations, and for general faculty morale.

SYKES: At Lansing Community College, division deans are academic leaders, senior level administrators whose levels of complexity on the job are monitored by the union. The more complex the division of responsibility or focus [is], the greater [is the] number of supervisors required by the union. They are contracted as supervisors because the union says that union members cannot supervise their members. Thus their leadership is derived from the union definition of supervision. Division deans have responsibilities to see that the operation and supervision of programs, faculty, and students works. They are involved in making policy and procedures as members of the president's cabinet and they are responsible for communicating and supervising their subordinates. They ensure [that] the college machine runs smoothly; they see to scheduling, hiring, curriculum, personnel, discipline, and complaints.

MULDER: I make my remarks as an ex–community college president. At Lake Michigan College, where I was president, the chair was a first-line administrator who was nominated from faculty ranks. In my opinion, chairs have the world's most difficult roles because while they are faculty and representative of faculty, they are also administrators and representative of administration. From the faculty perspective there is one view; often from the administrative side there is another diverging point of view. Conflict seems inevitable. The college must provide chairs with a strong support base that allows them to make decisions where the action occurs, at their level. This means [that] the college provides chairs with clear policy so that decision making can occur at many administrative levels consistently.

MESSINA: The old definition of division chairs was people who were collectively defined by their discipline; we had fourteen to sixteen chairs. But there was a problem: these chairs were also in a collective bargaining unit. How could a chair be effective if he were in the same bargaining unit as faculty in his academic department? Therefore, at Burlington we consolidated responsibilities in academic areas. Now two deans—one in science, technology, and math and the other in liberal arts—have overall responsibility to review curriculum and to evaluate full- and part-time faculty. None of the administrators have faculty rank; they are administrators who serve at the pleasure of the vice president, president, or board.

THORNTON: At Cuyahoga we do not have chairs of individual departments. Midlevel management here means deans of academic disciplines and program coordinators. Her division, such as liberal arts or humanities, defines a dean, and her main duties include evaluation, scheduling, and hiring. In particular, the dean's evaluation duty separates her from faculty. A department head or division chair is quasi-administrative, neither administrator nor faculty; we feel it is better to assign one role to midlevel management at Cuyahoga—administrator. This administrator leads from the middle—a crucial leadership position in the college.

Question 2. *What are the duties and roles of the community college chair?*

Cameron gave the most exhaustive list of chair duties. The other presidents categorized the duties of midlevel management into the following areas: curriculum and program review, class scheduling, evaluation, hiring, budgeting, faculty professional development, liaison to community, and supervision of office and staff. Lombardi (1974) suggested that the difference in detailing duties and responsibilities depends on whether a college is unionized or not. Colleges with unions had fewer duties or categories of duties, while nonunion colleges had a long list of duties. North Carolina is a right-to-work state. According to Cameron, Guilford Technical College spent months conducting a DACUM, a round-robin process of collecting, analyzing, and agreeing as a group on measures that elicited the following list of midlevel management duties:

- Scheduling and controlling work assignments, including determining course offerings and preparing individual teaching schedules
- Maintaining adequate (day and night) staff, including preparing newspaper advertisements, interviewing, recommending the hiring of new employees, providing orientation and training for new faculty and staff, supervising the instructional programs to ensure that program objectives are met, and providing necessary materials, orientation, and training to full-time and adjunct staff
- Attending meetings representing the department and holding meetings in a timely manner with the department
- Handling all aspects of registration, including but not limited to assigning faculty duties
- Working with appropriate personnel to develop desired student outcomes—usually by developing a DACUM chart
- Maintaining current course syllabi for all departmental courses in accordance with competencies from the departmental DACUM chart
- Working with faculty to maintain current instructional equipment and supplies
- Working with faculty to provide professional development opportunities
- Working with retention activities at the college, divisional, and departmental levels
- Recommending individuals to the college president for appointment to advisory committees
- Scheduling, conducting, and maintaining minutes of advisory committee meetings

- Marketing the college and the department to service area businesses, high schools, and other educational institutions in the area
- Recruiting students
- Preparing appropriate program materials in conjunction with other college staff
- Preparing program reviews for presentation to the board of trustees
- Handling student, faculty, and staff grievances in a professional manner
- Visiting classes to observe the quality of instruction and working with those instructors who need assistance to improve instructional methods
- Working with faculty and staff to meet deadlines for preparation and submission of required documents (such as preliminary rolls, 30 percent forms, grade sheets, payroll, new faculty, files, and others)
- Preparing, implementing, and controlling budgets
- Preparing evaluations of faculty and staff in the department and recommending pathways to achieve any needed improvement
- Working with faculty to select and approve textbooks consistent with course competencies
- Promoting a positive feeling toward the department and college in the community
- Projecting course enrollments in order to provide adequate classroom space and to order textbooks and materials
- Providing leadership for academic and career guidance activities
- Supporting institutional activities
- Serving on assigned institutional committees
- Working as an instructor (for example, preparing classes, maintaining good student relations, conducting classes, preparing teaching and assessment materials)

QUESTION 3. *What are the reporting structures for chairs at your college?*

As midlevel managers, deans report either to a vice president (division deans at Richland College and academic deans at Burlington County College) or a campus provost (division deans at Cuyahoga and Lansing Community Colleges). Some report to the executive cabinet, at least periodically, such as those at Burlington County College and Lansing Community College. As midlevel managers in the community college move from being called chairs, their status changes. They are consequently closer to upper-level management by at least one level of administrative rank, but all the presidents agreed that this position was "front line" to faculty and students. Thornton described these leaders as those "in the trenches"; Mulder described them as first-line administrators.

In most of the institutions represented here, division or academic deans may teach, usually one course and usually as adjunct faculty. Academic and division deans may have administrative assistants (usually a full-time faculty member) and their duties define release time. At Richland they are called faculty-teaching administrators, are discipline specific, and have twelve-month contracts. One responsibility they may have is to mentor adjunct or part-time faculty. At Lansing Community College, division deans have academic team leaders and directors of various programs. Cuyahoga deans are aided by program directors.

QUESTION 4. *How do you describe the need for midlevel management in your community college?*

Described as the "balkanized" position of colleges and universities, the chair is seen as being squeezed between faculty need and upper-level administrative need. Although chair duties are many and diverse and the expectations for them are great, many observers, especially in business, have seen this role conflict as the reason for the chair's demise. In the paragraphs that follow, the presidents respond to the challenge of midlevel management roles. Each of them points out the conflict involved in the role of chair and at the same time describes the great need for the position.

CAMERON: The department chair deals on a daily basis with conflicting roles. Most colleges [in North Carolina] classify academic department chairs as instructors (faculty). The primary responsibility of an instructor is to teach and advise; thus the department chair teaches and advises. In addition, he or she prepares the master class schedule, assigns instructors to classes, divides advising responsibilities, assigns faculty workload, and works with other department heads.

As an administrator, the chair evaluates instructors even as he or she works as a colleague who shares instructional materials, classroom, and student stories. Balancing a dual role can create uncomfortable situations for the chair, faculty, and staff in the department. The chair deals with conflicts such as grievances, too, including student complaints about faculty, faculty-to-faculty grievances, and so on. More complicated still are perceptions about the chair's role. Usually the chair sees himself as faculty (except for pay or the need for administrative communication), higher level administrators see the chair as faculty, and faculty see the chair as administrator. This places the chair in a very vulnerable position. While uncomfortable and difficult, this is an essential role for leaders in community colleges.

THORNTON: As long as there is a strong delineation between faculty and administrative roles, we will need midlevel management. Schools that are successful at blurring the lines hold out promise, however. [Richard Alfred at the University of Michigan discusses this idea, and it is currently being implemented in the Maricopa Community Colleges.] Academic deans are still sandwiched between faculty and administration. They have the critical role of interpreting both sides of an issue, an argument, and an idea. They are the front-line workers for administration. Many times such administrators become gatekeepers, not innovators.

At Cuyahoga we are experimenting with innovation. We are interested in providing a conduit for ideas and thinking, for creativity. Organizationally we are sensitive, open, and accepting of new ideas and to providing pathways for those ideas to emerge. To encourage creativity, we have created a think tank for change, for new ideas. Cochaired by a faculty member and an administrator, the college and the foundation are funding the think tank. In the past many felt [that] new ideas were not getting focus, research, or examination. Now the think tank provides a catalyst for new ideas. The members are getting out among faculty to encourage new ideas, particularly about curriculum. They are responding to the statement, "If we did things this way. . . ." Our next step is to organize a think tank for staff.

SYKES: In the best of all worlds it might be nice to function without midlevel managers. Those persons closest to the main business of the college—students— could simply make decisions within the confines of the vision and mission of the college. The difficulty is we do not function in a perfect world. In a union culture, if the first-line supervisor has membership in the group he is trying to supervise, there is a problem. Walking the fine line between administrator and union member is difficult. Cultures of unions are critical to understand. Evaluation of peers is an embedded concept in unions; it is not allowed. Peer supervision causes standstills, disempowers the midlevel manager, and causes the midlevel manager to lose his importance to the organizational structure. Division deans are administrators because they have to make hard, unpopular decisions.

MITTELSTET: It is absolutely impossible to eliminate midlevel management when faculty [are] on nine-month contracts. Colleges are year-round institutions and we count on midlevel managers to keep everything going. More importantly, the division dean plays a huge role in keeping the curriculum current and in new program exploration. These people meet and respond to critical needs in the community for courses and programs, they assess and launch countywide surveys to determine community support of new curricula or programs. They develop and involve advisory committees and keep their administrative colleagues informed.

For example, one such new program is the fast track for courses. Now a course can be completed in four weeks; students can enroll for two courses every four weeks, completing a two-year degree in one year. This idea came about after a study of weekend classes where it was determined that retention was significantly higher than in semester-long classes. The longer the semester, the higher the dropout rate. We paid attention. [The program is] now in its second year of a five-year plan for fast-track courses; seven-hundred students are enrolled. The most interesting factor of this new program is that the model seems excellent for at-risk students as well. No matter [what] the risk (family, work, children), a four-week class is easier to plan for and complete.

MESSINA: Midlevel managers in community colleges will always be needed because of the complexity of the institution. The issue of accountability provides a good example. If ADA [Americans with Disabilities Act] policies are conformed to, then who brings the sign language teacher to class for the deaf student? This implies management training and development, including on-the-job training. Colleges have an obligation for the professional development of their midlevel managers. The old idea of the department head being squeezed from the bottom and the top is eliminated if one takes midlevel managers out of the role of faculty; faculty has its own voice. Once midlevel managers are in place and have training, it is incumbent upon upper-level management to support them, especially when the going gets tough. In order to learn not to make mistakes on faculty contracts, midlevel managers review, observe, and learn the contract system—here's what it is, here's how to handle it, here's who can help. When grievances occur, capricious behavior cannot be attributed to the faculty supervisor because there is a clear separation between administrators and faculty. [The union chair at Burlington County College is not considered faculty.]

QUESTION 5. *Describe the successes and difficulties of chairs in your college.*

The college presidents reflected on the successes that midlevel managers in their community colleges have brought to their institutions. In many cases, too, they discussed the problems associated with the position. Because the position of midlevel manager, chair, or dean is so central to the internal functioning of the college, it is a very stressful job.

MULDER: Often when I looked for a new position due to a vacancy, I saw the department chair as an effective interim. At the time I was president, Dick Alfred at University of Michigan was involved in training for department heads and his program was extremely helpful in teaching and learning management skills. One particular department head was able to serve later as both dean and vice president. I gained wisdom from him and wonderful ideas about effectiveness. He also offered me, at times, my fiercest opposition. I knew he was an influence broker; he needed good data quickly. I valued his opinions. Later, when we instituted Institutional Effectiveness, it was from a model program developed by him. The position, the department chair, is where real leadership in the community college can be found.

Because I needed to work with whomever the faculty had selected as department head, I had to pay attention to them, to keep them informed and up-to-date on college issues. From the department head . . . I learned that I only was playing a mind game with myself if I thought I was holding on to power. From them I learned to reexamine things from different perspectives.

CAMERON: The quality and cohesiveness of the learning environment [see O'Banion, 1997] is part of the crucial position of the chair. . . . The effective chair cultivates excellent working relations with instructors, students, student service and maintenance staff, administrative services, and senior administration. Chairs are in position to see all sides of most issues related to the primary responsibility of the college, that is, instruction. No other position within the college has the same level and frequency of contact with the entire college staff. As colleges move toward [being] a more learning centered environment, the role of the chair becomes even more critical as he or she provides leadership, encouragement, and assistance in this paradigm shift.

MITTELSTET: We count on our division deans. They keep the office and the college open. We are dependent on their leadership at the college and in the community.

QUESTION 6. *What are the essential skills of a chair at your college?*

Good communication skills were mentioned by each of the presidents.

MESSINA: Communication. A skilled leader is someone who conveys the direction of the college president and board to their faculty, never leaving surprise as an option. A good chair is also personable, someone who can engage the faculty without offending them. A skilled administrator makes faculty want to work at the institution, makes faculty happy, and cares.

MULDER: Communication with peers, subordinates, and superordinates. Budget understanding.

CAMERON: Curricular knowledge. An understanding of accreditation. Knowing how to meet state curriculum standards. Working with business and industry. Marketing of programs. Recruitment and retention of students. Communication skills are critical. So is trust. Good leadership skills are essential; these include consensus and team-building skills. Training regarding personnel issues such as hiring, sexual harassment, termination, working with the media, legislators, public relations, and fundraising. Knowledge of the national perspective of community colleges and higher education.

THORNTON: Good communication—constantly navigating murky waters. Organized, detailed—constantly working on detail work. Flexible—ability to do diverse tasks simultaneously; ability to handle complex tasks. Credible—among faculty, demonstration of experience, that they have been there, they have taught.

Conclusion

Chairs.and those who serve in midlevel management positions retain a strong hold on the organizational hierarchy of community colleges. None of the presidents included here could imagine a system without this critical position, which they have dubbed the "front-line position" at the college.

Some of them warned, however, of the likelihood of burnout and limited pathways for chairs and division deans. Some mentioned the difficulty in attracting faculty members to this level and offered alternatives—people who could serve in administrative support positions to aid the midlevel manager. For the present time however, well-trained, informed chairs and deans are needed by these institutions to provide the foundation for moving colleges ahead academically. The guarantees for the future are not as forthcoming as some present-day chairs would expect. The likelihood of replacing chairs is being discussed, considered, and weighed by some of the presidents.

This discussion is a snapshot of the thought and consideration given to questions posed by the editor to college presidents in various locales in the United States. Neither the questions nor the voices are exhaustive. A similar analysis could be made at other institutions, and with other constituencies, such as faculty or the chairs themselves.

References

Lombardi, J. *The Department/Division Chairman: Characteristics and Role in the Community College.* Topical paper no. 40. Los Angeles: ERIC Clearinghouse for Community Colleges, May 1974.

O'Banion, T. *A Learning College for the 21st Century.* Phoenix: Oryx Press, 1997.

ROSEMARY GILLETT-KARAM *is president, Louisburg College, Louisburg, North Carolina.*

DONALD W. CAMERON *is president, Guilford Technical Community College, North Carolina.*

ROBERT C. MESSINA, JR., *is president, Burlington County College, New Jersey.*

STEPHEN K. MITTELSTET *is president, Richland College, Texas.*

ANNE E. MULDER *is past president, Lake Michigan College, Michigan, and professor at Nova Southeastern University, Florida.*

ABEL B. SYKES, JR., *is president, Lansing Community College, Michigan.*

JERRY SUE THORNTON *is president, Cuyahoga Community College District, Ohio.*

A grassroots movement responds to the training needs of community and technical college chairpersons.

The Need for Leadership Training: The Evolution of the Chair Academy

Gary L. Filan

Historically, leadership training has been designed for community college presidents, vice presidents, and deans to prepare them for a presidency. Few if any opportunities have been available to chairs, who outnumber all other types of administrators combined. Unlike the private sector, which devotes a considerable percentage of its training dollars to midlevel managers, community and technical colleges provide minimal or no funds to their midlevel leaders. Although the chair position is widely regarded as key to the effective functioning of a college's major academic and career programs, those filling the positions generally receive little or no formal training for the job. The department chairs of the Maricopa Community Colleges, located in the Phoenix metropolitan area of Arizona, recognized this need for training and were determined to identify the support and resources needed to obtain the necessary skills to lead their departments effectively.

The grassroots movement begun by these department chairs evolved into the current Chair Academy. These chairs recognized the need for skills-based training that would assist them with their complex roles and responsibilities in serving as the academic and administrative leaders in their respective departments. Due to the unique roles and missions of community and technical colleges and their open-door policy, chairs need training that can provide them with the skills needed to serve the growing number of first-generation college students, the underprepared students, and the increasing numbers of adult students, as well as students enrolled in certificate, transfer, and occupational programs.

While I was serving as the organizational development specialist for the Maricopa Community College District, I was contacted by these chairs in 1990 with a request for funds to attend a department chair training conference in Orlando, Florida. The Maricopa chairs hoped that by attending this conference they would receive information to use as a foundation and first step toward better understanding the complexities associated with their position. However, not only did the conference reinforce their need for skills-based training, it also made them aware that the conference was geared more toward department chairs at a university level rather than at a community college level. This group of community college chairs, upon their return to Arizona, decided to begin the research and design of a conference specifically geared toward department chairs at the community and technical college level. The seeds were planted for the Chair Academy, an organization that would come to provide comprehensive leadership training and development programs as well as services for leaders in postsecondary education worldwide.

Importance of Training for Chairs

Substantive operational and instructional issues within community colleges are taken care of at the department level. Therefore, department chairs are crucial to the success of the institution. The chair also is relied on by the administration to see that decisions are communicated and acted on. Chairs are often overworked, however, and underprepared for their jobs. Considering that this position is the most critical unit in the institution, the value of providing leadership training for chairs is too great not to invest in. Both administrative and academic leadership perspectives are needed to meet the challenges facing higher education (Gmelch and Miskin, 1993).

The importance of training chairs in the skills needed for the position is more crucial now than ever before because of the large-scale retirements in the ranks of faculty and chairs that will occur in the next decade. As current academic leaders retire, new ones will need to be developed. The chair position is the logical focus for training the next generation of college executive leaders. National and regional workshops are conducted for new presidents as well as for vice presidents and deans interested in becoming presidents to assist them with the roles and responsibilities associated with this top administrative position. However, prior to the formation of the Chair Academy in 1992, few such opportunities were available to community and technical college department chairs, who outnumber all other administrators (Tucker, 1992).

Chairs are typically thrust into positions that require behaviors considerably different from those they practiced as faculty members. Three of the most difficult aspects of the job are learning how to shift one's loyalty from a specific discipline to the institution as a whole, developing the skills to resolve conflicts, and knowing how to build an effective team whose members respect one another and appreciate differences. Unfortunately, few community and technical colleges provide any kind of formalized training to assist either their new or experienced chairs to develop these academic and administrative skills.

The chair sits in a precarious position, straddling the proverbial fence in serving two major roles: the middle manager–administrator and the faculty member–advocate. Performing both roles simultaneously can cause a great deal of difficulty in providing academic and administrative leadership for the department (Lucas, 1989). Those chairs who lean toward representing a broad-based institutional perspective are often perceived as selling out to the administration; those who tie their loyalty to the specific interests of department faculty are perceived as incapable of making tough decisions or otherwise advocating improvements or changes in curriculum, teaching methodologies, or related policies. Chairs have been recognized as the critical link between the administration, faculty, staff, programs, and students (Waltzer, 1975). "Department chairs in colleges and universities might feel somewhat distant from the boardrooms and executive suites of large corporations. But they face challenges and opportunities for leadership not unlike those confronting the managers of industry and commerce" (Seagren, Creswell, and Wheeler, 1993, p. 26). Chairpersons will be required to play an even more critical role in the next century in helping to provide leadership not only for their departments but also for their colleges. "An institution can run for a long time with an inept president but not for long with inept chairpersons" (Peltason, 1984, p. xi).

This balancing act can be exacerbated by the presence of collective bargaining, which draws clear distinctions between those in the bargaining unit and those outside it. Chairs need to have the trust and loyalty of both parties to be effective leaders. This balancing act of serving dual roles is difficult to accomplish, however, especially with little or no preparation for the position (Tucker, 1992). "Chairs must understand the political forces and processes of the institution and must skillfully maneuver groups and coalitions to achieve the autonomy and control necessary to develop a strong department" (Seagren, Creswell, and Wheeler, 1993, p. iv).

National Needs Assessment of the Community College Department Chair

One of the first tasks that the group of chairs who attended the Orlando conference and I carried out was to design and distribute a national survey of chief instructional officers (CIOs) in community and technical colleges. The survey asked CIOs to describe some of the key characteristics of the department chair position and to identify the leadership training needs of the position. In February 1991, the survey was distributed to twelve hundred community college CIOs in the United States. Responses were received from 426 colleges, or approximately 35 percent of the twelve hundred CIOs.

The principal finding of the survey was that fully 70 percent of the respondents, representing more than three hundred colleges, indicated that no formalized training was provided for their department chairs. In addition, the great majority of all colleges—both those that provided some training for the chairs and those that did not—indicated a strong interest in implementing training for their chairs on a wide range of topics. In addition, 50 percent of the responding CIOs said that faculty served in the role as chair, while only 19 percent were classified as administrators, and 31 percent of the colleges used a combination of both faculty and administrators in the position. One-quarter of the chairs were elected and 72 percent were appointed, presumably by the college administration.

The leadership training areas that the CIOs perceived as having the greatest need were faculty evaluation, strategic planning and managing budgets, curriculum planning, conflict management, complexity of academic and administrative roles, communication skills, legal issues, time management, and implementing educational technology. These areas eventually served as the program foundation for the Chair Academy's first international conference.

International Conference

With financial support from Paul A. Elsner, chancellor of the Maricopa Colleges, the grassroots group and I began to meet on a weekly basis to plan for an international conference specifically designed for community and technical college department chairs. As the district's organizational development manager, I was the only administrator in this group.

The committee knew that if we were to be successful we would have to design a conference that was completely different from the other conferences we all had attended throughout our professional careers. The following elements are still the cornerstone of the design of our annual conference (the 1999 event will be our eighth international conference).

Learner-centered. All concurrent and roundtable sessions (lasting one and a half hours) are designed to involve participants in discussions and activities. Presenters are asked to devote no more than thirty minutes to the key concepts and principles of their topic. This presentation is followed by group participation that draws on the knowledge and experiences of the participants and concludes with a short wrap-up. There is no theater-style seating anywhere in the conference. Roundtables are used extensively to allow for greater interaction and networking among participants.

Discipline-specific. Participants have the opportunity to meet with other deans or chairs in their respective areas to further discuss specific discipline and administrative issues pertinent to their jobs. This session occurs on the first day of the conference to allow participants to network throughout the remaining days with colleagues who are in similar positions.

Topic relevance. Concurrent sessions and roundtable discussions presented during the conference are selected based on their immediate relevance to educational leadership. Emphasis is placed on the roles and responsibilities associated with the chair, dean, and other midlevel administrative positions in the community and technical college setting.

Conference proceedings. All presenters, including keynote speakers, are asked to submit a paper related to their presentation. These papers are distributed in a notebook or on computer disk to each participant. These papers provide participants with the opportunity to review all of the topics and presentations of the conference, especially those sessions they are unable to attend, and to follow up with presenters if more information is desired.

Social activities. Any good conference requires an array of social activities that allow for plentiful networking opportunities. A dessert social prior to the start of the conference is followed the next day by a theme dance and college T-shirt exchange, and the conference concludes with a sit-down luncheon.

College hosts. Each year the Chair Academy contacts the community and technical colleges in the area where the conference is being held to recruit volunteers to act as hosts. Their hosting efforts not only provide local support and help in running the conference, but also allow the local institutions to showcase special programs and activities to an international audience.

National Study of Community and Technical College Chairs

Although community and technical college administrators (Moore, Twombly, and Martorana, 1985) and department chairs in universities (Seagren, Creswell, and Wheeler, 1993) have been studied in past national surveys, very few efforts have focused solely on the department chair in a community and technical college setting. The Chair Academy in 1992 recognized the importance of collecting additional data to fill this void. During the spring of 1992, the Chair Academy contacted Alan Seagren, professor and director of the Center for the Study of Higher and Postsecondary Education (CSHPE) at the University of Nebraska–Lincoln to help develop a survey to be distributed to department chairs in the United States and Canada. Seagren, his colleagues, and the CSHPE had conducted previous work in leadership development and in the study of department chairs at four-year institutions.

The survey was designed with the following purposes in mind: develop a profile of the characteristics of department chairs, instructional units, and institutions; identify implications for leadership development; and identify areas for future study and understanding of the chair position (Seagren and others, 1994). The survey was distributed to more than nine thousand department chairs in the United States and Canada in the fall of 1992. The survey collected data in four main areas: the characteristics of the chair, the responsibilities of the position, the challenges of the position, and the response strategies used by chairs.

A total of 3,000 surveys were returned, including 2,875 usable returns, yielding a response rate of 32 percent. The results provided the first comprehensive study of the position of department chair in community and technical colleges. The study also provided us with the information we needed to ensure that the appropriate leadership training topics as well as the administrative and academic needs of department chairs in community and technical colleges were going to be addressed through Chair Academy initiatives.

The survey indicated that 47 percent of department chairs were between forty-five and fifty-four years of age. Fifty-nine percent were male and 97 percent had prior experience as faculty members. Fifty-five percent of chairs reported that they had received release time from one or two classes per semester, and 97 percent reported that their appointments were renewable.

The following results have also been used for the design and development of other programs and services offered to department chairs:

More than 90 percent rated the following items "very important" or "impor-tant": planning, work environment, curriculum selection and feedback to faculty, communication, personal and professional goals, and professional development for faculty.

More than 98 percent indicated that ten of the twelve skills included in the survey were "very important" or "important": problem analysis, judgment, organizational ability, decisiveness, leadership, sensitivity, stress tolerance, oral communication, written communication, and educational values.

More than 90 percent "strongly agreed" or "agreed" to four out of thirty-six job challenges faced by chairs: maintaining program quality, strengthening the curriculum, maintaining a high-quality faculty, and changing the curriculum in response to technological development.

More than 66 percent indicated "strongly agree" or "agree" in response to twelve out of twenty-four strategies included in the survey: having planning and mission statements; analyzing employment trends; allocating financial resources; seeking external funding; participating in conferences for chairs; clarifying the role and responsibility of the chair; providing professional development programs for chairs, faculty, and staff; building partnerships with business; establishing networks with other chairs; and seeking a bal-ance between personal and professional activities for the chair.

The Academy for Leadership Training and Development

In addition to designing the first annual international conference developed solely for department and division chairs and deans, the department chairs of the Maricopa Community Colleges also began to research and design a pro-gram to provide department chairs with in-depth, skills-based training in the areas of academic and administrative leadership. These efforts eventually devel-oped into the Academy for Leadership Training and Development, which now offers leadership training to community and technical colleges throughout the United States and Canada as well as abroad.

Data from the 1992 national survey, as well as the ninety-seven chair activities discovered by the University of Nebraska's CSHPE research team (Creswell and others, 1990) and the fifty-four tasks and duties cited in Alan Tucker's (1992) landmark book *Chairing the Academic Department,* provided the academic and administrative leadership training topics to be addressed through the academy.

In the summer of 1992, the pilot program of the Academy for Leadership Training and Development was conducted in Prescott, Arizona. Participants came from community and technical colleges across the United States and Canada. The pilot program, along with one more offered the following summer, served as the basis for developing one of the most comprehensive leadership training and development programs in all of higher education designed specifically for organizational leaders within community and technical colleges.

The academy is a year-long, skills-based leadership development program that begins with a five-day learner-centered workshop, followed by a year-long practicum experience. The practicum is designed to provide participants with the opportunity to implement an Individualized Professional Development Plan (IPDP), a mentorship component, reflective practice and journaling, and a concluding five-day workshop. In addition, participants subscribe to a listserv that provides additional leadership information and support. The listserv also allows participants to continue interacting and sharing ideas with one another beyond the five-day workshop. Topics include but are not limited to the following: the complex role of the transformational leader, understanding behavioral work styles, leading in a time of change, building effective work teams, strategic and scenario planning, managing conflict effectively, creating learner-centered organizations, the leader's role in staff development, performance review, leading part-time staff, managing and leading technology, and encouraging and managing diversity.

There also are a number of themes that serve as the foundation for the leadership academy program: "Know thy self, know thy organization"; "Appreciate, value, and respect differences"; building a learning community; continuous improvement; transformational leadership; reflective practice and journaling; and "You can make a difference."

These themes, along with the leadership topics and practicum experience, have resulted in a program that has achieved an exemplary level of success both nationally and internationally. From the first two pilot programs, the Academy for Leadership Training and Development has expanded its offerings into Australia and is in the planning stages of implementing programs in Europe. By the end of summer 1999, more than one thousand participants will have graduated from the program.

What's Next in the Evolution of Leadership Development

The Chair Academy has developed several initiatives that address impending changes in the community college.

On-Line Leadership Development Course Offerings. In the spring of 1999, the Chair Academy, through its Academy for Leadership Training and Development Program, will begin offering the first in a series of on-line professional leadership development courses. Our first course offering is titled

"Effective Communication for Educational Leaders." The course is designed to be learner-centered and allows for a great deal of interaction among the participants. An electronic bulletin board will provide participants with the opportunity to share practical, effective communication solutions and strategies they have tried to implement in relationship to the on-line course. We anticipate that by the spring of 2000 we will have at least three more leadership courses on-line.

Customized and Statewide Succession and Leadership Development Programs. As we examine the community college movement of the past thirty-five years and look at its rich history, we realize that the time is near when a significant number of our current leaders will be leaving our ranks due to retirement. Immediate action needs to be taken by colleges to identify and develop our future leaders. Community and technical colleges need to look at how they are going to "grow" their future successors internally.

It is important to develop an organizational culture in which a focus on succession becomes a hallmark of strategic leaders. Succession planning has all too often been regarded as a replacement issue, not a strategic responsibility to be shared among the organization's stakeholders. Leadership must consider succession from the outset.

The leader of the future must be a tireless, inventive, observant, risk-taking, and ever-hopeful builder and enabler of management and leadership teams within the college. If successful, the leader will have constructed teams that carry out the organization's vision, goals, and purpose. By working together, these teams will accomplish more than their individual members ever could, therefore proving once again that the sum is greater than the parts.

We are asking the present-day leadership of community and technical colleges to act as servant leaders and to plan for the succession and development of future leaders. As servant leaders, we can provide an environment in which faculty, staff, and management can learn and grow as they work and share together.

Through the Chair Academy's Academy for Leadership Training and Development Program, we can help community and technical colleges address the challenge of succession planning. Our goal is to become a catalyst for a systemic movement focused on developing the leadership skills needed by department chairs, deans, and other organizational leaders, which in turn will help posture community and technical colleges as a vital component of higher education in the twenty-first century.

Most community and technical colleges do not have a succession and leadership development plan in place. Over the past year the Chair Academy has been contacting individual colleges and states to discuss their interest in having a customized succession planning and leadership development program designed to meet their specific needs. We are already in discussion with fifteen states that have indicated an interest.

Special Note of Recognition

It should be noted that the following individuals' vision and determination created a grassroots movement that has evolved into an organization that offers leadership programs and services to community and technical colleges worldwide. Their contributions and leadership are appreciated and continue to serve as a foundation for the Chair Academy in pursuit of its mission to advance academic and administrative leadership:

Jack Peterson, chair, cultural science, Mesa Community College
Jo Wilson, associate dean, business and technology, Mesa Community College
Jim Ferguson, chair (retired), psychology, Mesa Community College
Richard Malena, faculty, reading, Phoenix College
Chuck Zontanos, former chair, Glendale Community College
Gilbert Gonzales, dean, information technology, Mesa Community College
Conrad Bayley, honors coordinator, Estrella Mountain Community College
Aaron James, faculty, life science, Mesa Community College

References

Creswell, J. W., Wheeler, D. W., Seagren, A. T., Egly, N. J., and Beyer, K. D. *The Academic Chairperson's Handbook.* Lincoln: University of Nebraska Press, 1990.

Gmelch, W. H., and Miskin, V. D. *Leadership Skills for Department Chairs.* Bolton, Mass.: Anker, 1993.

Lucas, A. F. "Motivating Faculty to Improve the Quality of Teaching." In A. F. Lucas (ed.), *The Department Chairperson's Role in Enhancing College Teaching.* New Directions for Teaching and Learning, no. 37. San Francisco: Jossey-Bass, 1989.

Moore, K. M., Twombly, S. B, and Martorana, S. V. *Today's Academic Leaders: A National Study of Administrators in Community and Junior Colleges.* University Park: Center for the Study of Higher Education, Pennsylvania State University, 1985.

Peltason, J. W. In A. Tucker (ed.), *Chairing the Academic Department: Leadership Among Peers.* (2nd ed.) New York: ACE/Macmillan, 1984.

Seagren, A. T., Creswell, J. W., and Wheeler, D. W. *The Department Chair: New Roles, Responsibilities and Challenges.* ASHE-ERIC Higher Education Report no. 1. Washington, D.C.: ASHE-ERIC, 1993.

Seagren, A. T., Wheeler, D. W., Creswell, J. W., Miller, M. T., and VanHorn-Grassmeyer, K. *Academic Leadership in Community Colleges.* Lincoln: University of Nebraska Press, 1994.

Tucker, A. *Chairing the Academic Department: Leadership Among Peers.* (3rd ed.) New York: ACE/Macmillan, 1992.

Waltzer, H. *The Job of Academic Department Chairman.* Washington, D.C.: American Council on Education, 1975.

GARY L. FILAN *is executive director of the Chair Academy, located at the downtown campus of Mesa Community College, Mesa, Arizona.*

*Effective leadership training for chairs needs to be situated in
realistic contexts. Formats that connect chairs to their actual work
environments include mentoring, action-learning projects, and
reality-based case studies.*

Situating Midlevel Managers' Training:
Learning and Doing in Context

John M. Pettitt

Community college professionals must develop sometimes delicate and sometimes aggressive approaches to negotiating progress toward goals among competing forces. As in any organization or community, choosing effective
approaches to this process may depend greatly on the context of the situation
(Deetz, 1992). The observation that context is critical to the job of the professional is the subject of this chapter. While it comments on the findings of a
study on North Carolina community college chairs (Hilton, 1997), efforts are
made to illustrate the need for training and learning situated in the context and
experiences of the college administrator known as the midlevel manager, chair,
or division dean.

Wilson (1993) is an adult educator who argues that context is central to
the understanding of adult cognition. He posits that we think and learn in
socially constructed settings that indicate to us the "tools" we need to accomplish our learning. Contextually, then, we say that no one can simply *train* for
the position of leadership in a community college; he or she must *do* the job
to know the job. Doing the job depends on thinking about the job, determining what to pay attention to, and planning to accommodate to the needs of
adults. Context helps us understand how learning and knowing are situated.
In the research reported here, an analysis of what community college chairs
do—that is, their discussion of the context of their jobs as department heads
in various colleges in North Carolina—is presented.

Community college chairs' leadership responsibilities, tasks, and training
needs may be interpreted in light of organizational and community contexts
in which issues of power, authority, current college initiatives, strategic and
policy changes, and the overall culture of the chair's college and community

affect what chairs must do and what they must learn in order to be effective in their work. For the purpose of this analysis, chair tasks and learning needs are separated into categories such as curriculum development, budgeting, professional development, personnel administration, and internal administration. These categories are intimately related within the organizational and community contexts just mentioned. For example, many chairs in this study identified a need to receive training in motivating faculty and evaluating faculty performance, but far fewer felt a need for training in making budget decisions. If training were to be based solely on these survey results, that is, disconnected from a particular chair's reality, a planner might design faculty performance and motivation training for chairs that is disassociated from budget issues. Faculty development and budgeting are inseparably linked for many chairs, however, depending on the power the chairs have over rewards such as merit pay or allocating other resources. These decisions also become influenced by the multiple responsibilities of the chair that include supporting the department faculty, serving administration's needs, upholding the mission of the college, and maintaining links to the community (Goldenburg, 1993). Therefore, an explicit theme for this chapter is that effective training based on interpretations of community college department chairs' expressed needs, such as those found in this study, cannot be conducted in formats that are isolated or disconnected from the chair's experiential world or the context of the situated reality. Suggestions are made to aid the chair in this endeavor. The chapter describes the chair study in detail to demonstrate the chairs' perceptions of their jobs.

Description of the Study

Initially conducted as dissertation research by Hilton (1997), information was collected from 131 department chairs and 363 faculty members within the North Carolina Community College System. Based on previous studies by Seagren and others (1994) and Gmelch and Miskin (1993), the chair survey asked respondents to indicate the tasks that were part of their job, the extent to which each task should be part of their responsibilities, and the extent to which they needed training in the area of each task. Although mention is made of the demographics and the chairs' perceptions of their tasks, attention is concentrated on the positing of training within the context and experiences of the chair.

Responding chairs were predominantly male (64 percent), appointed (94 percent) as opposed to elected, and white (94 percent); very few were African American (5 percent), Hispanic (1 percent), or Native American (.05 percent). Most were between forty and fifty-nine years old (84 percent), many held master's (77 percent) or doctoral (12 percent) degrees, and many had been in their current positions more than five years (68 percent). Most had been at their college more than ten years (21 percent) and many more than twenty years (40 percent). About 60 percent of the chairs taught classes ten hours or more per week and another 14 percent taught between six and nine hours per week; in addition, 89 percent reported working more than forty hours per week on average. A majority of the chairs (89 percent) were not seeking advancement, but 59 percent indicated that they would accept a higher position if it were offered. Chair tasks in curriculum and instruction, internal administration, professional development, human relations and personnel administration, budget planning and development, student relations and administration, and external administration are described briefly to show similarities and differences among the chairs.

Curriculum and instruction. The items in this category are related to leadership in planning, conducting, evaluating, and renewing curriculum and instruction within the department and as connected to the college's mission and strategic planning. Nearly all chairs reported involvement in establishing short-term goals and objectives (98 percent), establishing procedures for developing department goals and objectives (96 percent), analyzing department goals and objectives in relation to the mission and goals of the college (96 percent), encouraging the use of new instructional materials (96 percent), and establishing long-term department goals and objectives (95 percent). Reporting high levels of agreement, chairs demonstrated the relationship between having many years of experience in community colleges and their understanding and participation in planning keyed to the needs of students, faculty, and new programs.

Internal administration tasks. The items in this category reflect the leadership, management, and coordination of communications and resources within the department and between the department and the college. Nearly all chairs had responsibility for representing the department to administration (96 percent), increasing the use of computers for instruction (95 percent), delegating authority and responsibility for task completion (94 percent), utilizing committees for departmental functions (92 percent), and securing state-of-the-art technical equipment (92 percent). The fewest number of chairs viewed the personnel and human relations tasks of communicating with the affirmative action officer (64 percent) and promoting greater gender equity (57 percent) as part of their job. Less than half of the chairs thought that these tasks should be a considerable part of their job.

Learning how to increase the use of computers for instruction and to secure state-of-the-art technical equipment were seen by chairs as the first and third highest needs among all seventy-seven tasks identified in the instrument. In concert with these priorities, the second highest need identified among all the tasks was also an internal administration item related to computers and technology: the task of utilizing computer services for departmental management. In addition, most chairs also reported a need for training in the areas of using quality management techniques and mediating faculty complaints for the administration.

Professional development tasks. Nearly all chairs (96 percent) were active in and felt responsible for their own professional development and for supporting their faculty's professional development. Only about half the chairs, however, provided any professional development experiences for faculty. Most chairs also were engaged in and wanted training in motivating faculty and staff. Closely related to activities in motivating faculty was a need by most chairs for training in assessing and providing feedback to faculty.

Human relations and personnel administration tasks. Chairs indicated that they were highly involved in the tasks of identifying personnel needs for their department (96 percent), interviewing prospective faculty (95 percent), reviewing credentials of applicants (95 percent), evaluating the performance of professional staff (90 percent), and (to a lesser extent) recruiting new faculty (88 percent). Only the task of evaluating the performance of professional staff, however, was seen by most of the chairs as an area in which they needed training. In addition, most chairs expressed a need for training that would help them improve their skills in making decisions concerning faculty retention and release. Looking at both professional development and personnel administration findings together, a logical interpretation might be that chairs do not have great difficulty matching faculty strengths to the goals of the department and the college, but they are sometimes met with difficulties maintaining effectiveness in reaching these goals.

Budget planning, development, and control tasks. Chairs demonstrated a high level of responsibility for preparing and explaining department budget requests (94 percent), planning expenditures (92 percent), and deciding priorities (90 percent) for the department budget. In contrast, preparing and monitoring a system for all department expenditures, a task that was less prevalent among the chairs' actual responsibilities (77 percent) and which about 75 percent thought should at least be a considerable part of their responsibilities, was the only responsibility for which most chairs wanted at least some training. These chairs appear for the most part to have had little difficulty in making decisions about how money should be spent to reach department and college goals, but they did need help in tracking how expenditures were effective and efficient in reaching these goals.

Student relations and administration tasks. This category included some of the lowest involvement rates, with less than half the chairs engaged in supervising student file maintenance, making admissions decisions concerning individual students, and supervising advisement and counseling programs for students with student problems and complaints. The task with the highest involvement by chairs in this area, responding to the needs of a wider range of students, was also identified as a training need by most chairs. Chairs also revealed the need for faculty to receive additional training in student advising and counseling programs, especially because student complaints focus on poor faculty response and sensitivity in these areas. Two of the tasks considered by the faculty to be very important for the chairs were communicating faculty needs to administration and improving the departmental image and reputation; the faculty perceptions of chairs were usually externally oriented, and neither program nor student oriented.

External administration tasks. This category displayed one particular item, that of representing the department to the public, among the tasks in which nearly all chairs had responsibility. Less than half of the chairs were engaged in soliciting grants and outside funds, contacting prospective employers for graduates, and conducting follow-up studies on graduates. Even fewer chairs thought that these three tasks should be a considerable part of their jobs. In contrast, most chairs wanted at least some training in soliciting grants and outside funds.

Discussion

Apparently chairs are committed to the mission of the community college; they do not feel that they have any difficulty interpreting the mission in relation to their tasks. Indeed, most of the chairs have been part of the community college system for a major portion of their adult lives. Consequently there is reason to assume that they operate primarily from a commitment to this mission and not from other ambitions; for example, they did not seek advancement. Other commitments to administration, their fellow faculty, and the community must be viewed in light of what the mission and vision for the future of the community college means to these chairs within their personal and social contexts. For example, these chairs and faculty for the most part did not see grants and fundraising as a responsibility that should be a great part of a chair's job, yet they wanted training in it. This need for training appears to be influenced by the context of the chairs' perceived realities for the present and future and not by their wishes for an ideal job description. Better data gathering over time that measures trends and needs should be part of the chairs' research for doing their jobs effectively. These data can be used to modify and develop the departmental vision.

Developing and maintaining a departmental vision that matches the college's mission and vision for the future could be a powerful driving force in how these chairs view their job. The chairs may see their strongest needs in relation to developing the intellectual, human, and material resources required to build a present-day structure that will meet the demands of the community and the community college as the present continually moves into the future.

Chairs are committed to their own development in

Learning how to keep their departments moving into the future technologically, for the purposes of department management and instruction

Providing leadership to faculty in a manner that will enhance their performance in the classroom and their shared leadership in maintaining the department's effectiveness in fulfilling the college's mission and vision for the future

Creating a system for short-term and long-term curriculum development that will support their understanding of the mission of the community college and its future

Giving leadership to developing a support system within and outside the department that can keep up with an ever-changing and diverse student population

Mediating or developing systems for mediating conflict among students, faculty, and administrators (conflict can be seen as a problem or as part of the growth process in the college's rapidly changing environment)

Managing and developing (though possibly reluctantly developing) the financial resources needed for the department to maintain and enhance its ability to carry out its role in the community college's mission and vision for the future of serving its community's needs

Implications for the Design of Community College Department Chair Leadership Training

Although general mission statements of community colleges may be very similar, the strategic plans and visions generated by that mission find meaning in the realities of the college and community contexts, histories, and cultures. For the department to be a viable part of seeing that mission and vision become realities in the future, the chair must make decisions among alternatives that exist within his or her present day realities. Therefore, to meet the training needs of chairs, colleges may need to consider not only the skills and knowledge that are needed but also how they are to be used to negotiate among sometimes cooperating and sometimes competing forces such as administration, faculty, students, and community.

To do this, training may need to be designed that is situated in the context and experiences of the chair and that is problem solving in nature. This approach to training allows what is learned to be holistic and blended with the experiences and work of the learner—in this case, the department chair. The following paragraphs give examples of this approach.

For department chair training to be situated, the learning experience must at the very least allow for the chair's reality to be a part of the learning experience, if not to be the learning experience itself. Situated learning involves the development of mental schemas "that involve role, relationship, and legitimate participation in a community's work" (Pratt and Associates, 1998, p. 88). In contrast with what is sometimes described as traditional classroom learning, situated learning does not involve well-defined problems with specific right and wrong solutions. Rather, the total environment of the activity affects situated learning that results from authentic activity, such as the work of the department chair—that is, the community of work for that department chair. Environmental factors might include the accountability of the learner to those in power or those who should have power, the tools that are specific to the task, the resources that are or are not available, the overall physical and emotional environment of the situation, and the many other factors that the chair knows, based on her or his experience, can affect the situation in which she or he is learning (Brown, Collins, and Duguid, 1989). Chairs cannot learn or master the skills they need to further the mission and vision of the college and community if the acquisition of those skills are disconnected from all of the forces and elements that interact in their particular jobs. In addition, they are already masters of much of their job and will bring these skills to bear on new areas of interest. Situated learning theory suggests that learning about tracking budgets, motivating faculty, or selecting computer hardware and software have no meaning without taking into account these factors, especially the political nature of their roles and their relationships with administration, other departments, and the larger community.

Training formats that connect chairs to their reality may include mentoring, action-learning projects, or reality-based case methods. A limited but useful example of the importance of situated learning emerged recently in a class that emphasizes exploring how we make effective decisions about instructional strategies. As part of the course, participants conduct a self-directed learning project with two required parameters. First, the project must be about instructional strategies and the decisions made about such strategies, and second, it must have some connection to the "real world."

A community college administrator in a middle-management position was very concerned that her responsibility was to give leadership to others, mostly part-time faculty, with responsibility for instruction; she was not to be an instructor herself. After some discussion we decided that she could examine her own job by using self-directed learning. She would, by including her faculty, examine her own roles as coach, facilitator, and mentor. This might give her a chance to look at her own job from a perspective she had not previously used. The purpose of this self-examination was to reflect on and reveal what she was learning from her work, not to learn how to apply to her work abstract principles developed by someone else. Her faculty could participate as well by reflecting on her as coach, facilitator, and mentor. Together, as collaborative participants in the learning process, the administrator and the faculty would develop and work toward common goals and interests deriving from their explicit and felt needs. In fact, the group decided to work together to develop a mentor's guide for part-time faculty that included the expressed needs of the present faculty. Situated in the context of part-time faculty needs, the mentoring program promises to address and work within the context of needs expressed and activities needed to bring professional development and training to part-time faculty.

Situated learning suggests problem-solving environments. According to Wilson (1993), problem solving and the learning that results from it occur in real, or authentic, settings and are more than simple, specific mental processes. Although there are other motivations for learning than solving problems, the training priorities identified by the chairs in the study presented in this chapter appear to be related to problems needing to be solved, the resolution of which must support the mission and vision of their particular institution and community. There is a specific nature to these problems that makes problem solving, and therefore learning, dependent on that context. Training needs and problems connected to technology might be better served in one college by consultation or mentoring approaches that assist the chair in developing an actual technology plan for the department. In another college, however, these decisions might be made collegewide and the training response might address how the department would apply the selected technology infrastructure to its specific needs. In some colleges a chair might be able to be trained in grantsmanship focused on the specific resource development needs of her department, whereas resource development at other colleges or departments might be better served through partnerships with business and industry.

These problems are related to the resources and processes needed to realize the mission and vision of the chairs' institutions and departments. One way of expressing why this approach may be important is that a chair probably feels the need to have a process for involving her faculty in developing effective short-range and long-range goals for the department and that promote the mission and vision of the college. This is different from saying that a chair wants knowledge of a particular model or to acquire a set of predetermined skills. This is not to say that certain models and skills will not be helpful, but that they must at least be tested and adapted within the chair's context, if not learned directly from that context.

Summary

Within the existing structure of many community colleges, chairs are critical to the college's effectiveness in carrying out its mission and realizing its vision for the future. The chairs in the study presented in this chapter are very likely aware of this responsibility and accept it because of their commitment to the community college mission and vision. They see their roles as giving leadership to the curriculum development process for their department. Inherent to this process is its connection to the college's mission and vision. The chairs work to develop the intellectual, human, material, and political resources needed to support the delivery of the curriculum to diverse audiences and, consequently, to fulfill their college's mission and vision. Their training needs are related to being as effective as possible in making their departments a viable part, if not a leader, in this fulfillment. These are real situations and real problems for these department leaders. This reality requires the real learning and real solutions offered by connecting training to their specific situations.

References

Brown, J., Collins, A., and Duguid, P. "Situated Cognition and the Culture of Learning." *Educational Researcher,* 1989, *18* (1), 32–41.

Deetz, S. "Departmental Leadership and Departmental Culture." In L. Hickson and D. Stacks (eds.), *Effective Communication for Academic Chairs.* Albany: State University of New York Press, 1992.

Gmelch, W., and Miskin, V. *Leadership Skills for Department Chairs.* Bolton, Mass.: Anker, 1993.

Goldenburg, M. "Common and Uncommon Concerns: The Complex Role of the Community College Department Chair." In J. Bennett and D. Figuli (eds.), *Enhancing Departmental Leadership: The Roles of the Chairperson.* Phoenix: Oryx Press, 1993.

Hilton, H. "Department Chairs' Roles, Functions, and Needs for Professional Development in North Carolina's Community Colleges." Unpublished doctoral dissertation, North Carolina State University, 1997.

Pratt, D., and Associates. *Five Perspectives on Teaching and Learning in Adult and Higher Education.* Malabar, Fla.: Krieger, 1998.

Seagren, A. T., Wheeler, D. W., Creswell, J. W., Miller, M. T., and VanHorn-Grassmeyer, K. *Academic Leadership in Community Colleges.* Lincoln: University of Nebraska Press, 1994.

Wilson, A. "The Promise of Situated Cognition." In S. B. Merriam (ed.), *An Update on Adult Learning.* New Directions for Adult and Continuing Education, no. 57. San Francisco: Jossey-Bass, 1993.

JOHN M. PETTITT *is assistant professor, Department of Adult and Community College Education, North Carolina State University.*

Although popular and academic literature often distinguish leadership from management, the complex nature of the chair position requires competency in both areas. Leadership theories and emerging models can inform the practice of managerial leaders.

Understanding Managerial Leadership as More Than an Oxymoron

Erika Yamasaki

As several of the preceding chapters indicate, midlevel managers in the community college are often burdened with tensions resulting from their dual roles as administrators and faculty members. For chairs, deans, and others who aspire to be leaders as well as managers, the challenge is even greater. The staggering number and pressure of administrative tasks leaves little time for midlevel managers to attend to academic activities, let alone to provide departmental leadership.

When examining these multiple roles inherent in the midlevel manager's position, it is necessary to consider the differences between leading and managing. Often these terms are used synonymously, or leadership is associated with an organizational position. In the case of community colleges, the literature tends to consider presidents and upper-level administrators as the campus leaders. Rarely are midlevel managers included in this group, although this volume has clearly demonstrated the need for leaders in the middle ranks. To build on the concept of "leading from where you are," as Spaid and Parsons label it in Chapter Two, this chapter considers how models and theories of leadership may guide midlevel managers in their practice of *managerial leadership.*

Moving Beyond the Either/Or Framework

A popular perspective on the differences between managers and leaders is summed up on the cover of Bennis and Nanus's (1985) *Leaders:* "Managers do things right. Leaders do the right thing." Although the intent of this framework is not to belittle anyone for doing things right, it tends to portray managers and their actions as ineffective. Managers are important and efficient, but leaders are effective.

Although Rost (1985) acknowledges that some managers are also leaders, he clearly distinguishes between the two. He characterizes leaders as being values driven, taking high risks, maintaining influential relationships with followers, looking to the future, and being intellectual. Managers, however, are described as being production driven, taking low risks, maintaining authoritative relationships with subordinates, focusing on the here and now, and being practical. Similarly, Zaleznik (1992) writes that managers tend to adopt impersonal or passive attitudes toward goals while leaders tend to participate actively in the formation of goals. Managers also are said to possess a survival instinct that supersedes the need for risk, unlike leaders, who will take risks where the opportunity for reward appears promising.

As with most frameworks that present either/or situations, this dichotomy does not adequately capture the realities of leadership and management, especially as they are needed and practiced in the community college. What is more useful is a consideration of how midlevel managers, such as department and division chairs, can also be leaders. That is, how can they be effective managerial leaders?

What Is Leadership?

To arrive at an understanding of effective managerial leadership it is necessary first to discuss what is meant by *leadership*. This is no easy endeavor considering that thousands of articles and books have been written about the topic. One common approach to this task is to examine the behaviors and practices of leaders.

In his landmark study of leadership, Burns (1978) writes that the characteristic that distinguishes leadership from management is purpose. That is, leaders act on the basis of group purpose and their intention is to enact real change. In most cases this change can be categorized as transformative, a condition leading Burns to coin the term *transformational leader*. Such a leader is able to raise followers to new levels of morality and motivation en route to mutually shared goals such as justice or equality.

Bennis (1989) identifies four leadership competencies based on his study of sixty corporate leaders and thirty public sector leaders. First, *management of attention* enables these individuals to draw others to them by demonstrating exceptional commitment. Through the second competency, *management of meaning,* they are able to communicate their vision and align others with them. *Management of trust* is essential in all organizations. The leaders in Bennis's study demonstrate reliability and constancy, which fosters others' trust in them. Finally, *management of self,* or the ability to know one's skills and to utilize them effectively, is identified.

After surveying more than five hundred corporate leaders, Kouzes and Posner (1991) conclude that there are five key leadership behaviors: leaders challenge the process, inspire a shared vision, enable others to act, model the way, and encourage the heart. These five categories of behaviors were measured by the thirty-item Leadership Practices Inventory, an instrument that allows for self-assessment as well as evaluation by others. Survey participants indicated on a scale of 1 (rarely) to 5 (always) their frequency of engaging in certain types of leadership behavior. Examples of questionnaire items include "I look for opportunities that challenge my skills and abilities," and "I give people freedom and responsibility to make their own decisions in this organization."

Bass and Avolio's (1994) continuum of leadership identifies the transformational leader as the most effective leader. This individual is able to achieve success by employing the "Four I's": idealized influence, inspirational motivation, intellectual stimulation, and individualized consideration. Although the other types of leadership identified, such as transactional and laissez-faire, are appropriate for certain situations, the transformational approach is considered optimal.

As these various models and frameworks illustrate, there is no consensus as to how to define or measure leadership. Birnbaum (1988), however, identifies five common approaches to studying organizational leadership: *trait theories* (such as the Great Man theory) emphasize the role of personality and individual characteristics, *behavioral theories* study what leaders do, *power and influence theories* (such as the transactional and transformational perspectives) consider the types and use of power as well as the ways leaders exercise influence over followers, *contingency theories* emphasize the importance of situational factors, and *symbolic and cultural theories* assume that organizational structures are created over time through participants' interactions. Bensimon, Neumann, and Birnbaum (1989) add one additional category, *cognitive theories,* which consider leadership as a social attribution. From this perspective, organizational success or failure is attributed to the leader.

In higher education, transformational leaders and their ability to initiate organizational change and raise followers to a new level of morality and motivation (Burns, 1978) have been praised. One "survival guide" for new chairs and deans even advises these individuals to utilize the tenets of transformational leadership as they act as institutional change agents (Hilosky and Watwood, 1997). The current impetus for community colleges to become learning organizations (Mellow, 1996; Myran, Zeiss, and Howdyshell, 1995; O'Banion, 1997) also has spawned a widespread call for leaders who can transform their institutions. These recent references to transformational leadership, however, tend to emphasize only its motivational or innovative aspects. The moral component indicated by Burns has been lost as the term has grown in popularity (Bensimon, Neumann, and Birnbaum, 1989).

What Are Managers to Do?

Amid the varying perspectives on leadership there is widespread agreement that unlike managers, leaders are not defined by their positions. For many midlevel managers in community colleges, however, their position will provide an opportunity—perhaps the first chance they have ever had at their institution—to lead. As Rost (1985) stated in his concluding comments at the Organization Development Network National Conference in San Francisco, "Some managers are leaders, others are not. All managers are not leaders and never will be. . . . the leaders who are middle managers [I call] *administrative leaders,*" (p. 13). He went on to say, "Managers who are leaders often engage in leadership behavior, but at other times engage in strictly management behavior. Managers who are leaders never act as leaders all the time in organizations. Their positions as managers prohibit such exclusive behavior patterns" (p. 13).

This inherent conflict facing administrative or managerial leaders is supported by the experiences and conclusions of other researchers. Furthermore, the situations of midlevel managers in community colleges are compounded by their third role as faculty members. Welch (1996) identifies three functions that chairs and deans perform in the community college: academic, managerial, and leadership. As leaders, chairs are looked to for motivation and vision. The potential pitfall identified by seasoned chairs and deans was the overwhelming number and urgency of their managerial tasks, leaving little time for leadership and academic activities. Hilosky and Watwood (1997) categorize the roles of chairs and deans into three similar themes: change leader, administrative manager, and college professional. Being a change leader encompasses nine roles, including being a change agent, facilitator, team player, communicator, and visionary. The six roles forming the administrative manager theme include being a planner, market agent, coordinator, and stabilizer. Educator and mentor are the two roles placed under the college professional theme. Of all the roles they identify, Hilosky and Watwood single out the change agent function as the most important for deans and chairs.

If, however, a chair or dean focuses on her role as a change leader while neglecting administrative tasks, she is likely to lose the trust and support of her colleagues. Once that happens, she can no longer be an effective leader or manager. Thus the situation is complex and precarious for midlevel managers who aspire to be managerial leaders. For them, effective management seems to be an integral component of successful leadership—although it might also be argued that an effective leader can inspire members of her department to a shared vision that in turn motivates them to pick up the slack when the chair falls behind in managerial tasks. This conceptualization of chairs as managerial leaders—a confluence of faculty, leader, and manager—needs further investigation. Neither the traditional leadership literature nor studies of community college presidents addresses the inherent conflicts of being a midlevel managerial leader. That is, the unique power and interpersonal relationships that surround collective bargaining issues as well as faculty-administration and student-faculty conflicts add dimensions not yet studied in this arena.

What Do New Models Offer?

The preceding chapters of this volume have provided both empirical evidence of midlevel managers' needs for professional development and descriptions of programs that provide learning opportunities. Although these initiatives at the institutional, district, and national levels can better prepare leaders and managers, the daily challenges are unlikely to subside. In all likelihood, the jobs of midlevel managers will grow more complex with the advent of the twenty-first century. Recent literature on the future of community colleges, and particularly on leadership for the new millennium, identifies an approaching era of great organizational change, even chaos (Rost, 1991; Myran, Zeiss, and Howdyshell, 1995; Mellow, 1996; Gibson-Benninger, Ratcliff, and Rhoads, 1995). As Spaid and Parsons write in Chapter Two, on learning to lead from the middle, a new leadership paradigm—one that is not hierarchical or centered on an individual—is necessary. Furthermore, leadership training programs will face the imperative to incorporate new perspectives and appropriate learning methods in order to foster effective managerial leaders.

How can this be accomplished? It comes as no surprise that numerous leadership models for the next century have already been proposed. Democratic, collaborative, community-based, and inclusive—these are but a few of the terms used to describe the new approach to leadership. The hallmark of the twenty-first-century leader will be that he or she will not exist; instead, there will be a leadership team. Leadership will no longer be an individual practice; rather, it will be a collaborative endeavor. Some examples from the literature are included here to demonstrate the common theme among various approaches.

Gibson-Benninger, Ratcliff, and Rhoads (1995) write that a fundamental challenge facing community college leaders is the creation of an environment in which a diverse group of students and staff can make positive contributions. This requires a democratic vision of leadership rather than the traditional, top-down, positional approach. They suggest that "the mission and identity of the college needs to be deeply rooted within the culture of the organization and this necessitates involving diverse faculty, staff, students, and community members in a more collaborative process" (p. 9). Critical aspects of this democratic approach include sensitivity to individual differences, a commitment to empowering diverse constituents, and an emphasis on team building.

These elements are similar to Rost's (1991) leadership paradigm for postindustrial society. This new framework embraces collaboration, diversity and pluralism in structures and participation, civic virtues, client orientation, and consensus-oriented policymaking processes. Because this work is not specific to higher education, it is clear that the need for inclusive and empowering leadership is not limited to a particular organization or field.

According to Mellow (1996), rigid hierarchical structures cannot provide adequate leadership for this era in which the proliferation of information technology and new knowledge requires organizations to change continuously. Given these dynamic conditions of the coming century, community colleges are advised to adopt a new structural model that will facilitate learning and transformation at the organizational level. Mellow believes that within these learning organizations chairs will play a critical leadership role by inspiring faculty to change, by encouraging communication, and by allowing their institutions to evolve.

In *Community College Leadership in the New Century,* Myran, Zeiss, and Howdyshell (1995) address not only learning organizations but also learning communities: "The new community college leadership model grows out of a new understanding of the place learning fills for people, organizations, and communities" (p. 4). Based on this understanding, they offer a leadership model for the new century that is both learner- and community-centered. Compared to the old leadership paradigm, the new model will focus on vision rather than on plans; will be empowering, not directing; will stress team rather than individual performance; will be inclusive of all constituents rather than exclusive; and will emphasize team building and collaboration rather than bureaucracy.

This sampling of leadership models for the new century demonstrates that despite some semantic differences and a distinguishing characteristic or two, they all espouse a common theme: effective leaders communicate and work as a team. These are not novel concepts, and herein lies one valuable lesson: leadership development programs should continue to stress fundamental leadership components in the new era of learning organizations. The more difficult questions facing us are, With *whom* should leaders communicate and work? and *How*? Answers to these queries are contingent upon the myriad changes faced by leaders and their institutions.

Conclusion

To succeed, managerial leaders both today and in the future will need to observe, reflect, assess, and respond to their changing organizational contexts continuously. Furthermore, they will need to look at themselves and do the same. Is this too much to ask of an individual who is already responsible for budgets, course scheduling, conflict mediation, personnel issues, curricular changes, and countless other administrative duties? Perhaps. But the outcomes of empowering staff and colleagues to be part of a leadership team, one responsible for daily operations as well as long-term visioning, might include the opportunity to delegate more of these managerial tasks.

Additionally, there is the matter of working with upper-level administrators and convincing them of the importance of the managerial leadership concept. Existing organizational structures and power relationships may impede midlevel managers from exercising leadership practices in the manner they desire. Their response to this challenge will be the true test of whether managerial leadership is an oxymoron or a realistic endeavor.

References

Bass, B. M., and Avolio, B. (eds.) *Improving Organizational Effectiveness Through Transformation Leadership*. Thousand Oaks, Calif.: Sage, 1994.

Bennis, W. "Why Leaders Can't Lead." *Training and Development Journal,* Apr. 1989, pp. 35–39.

Bennis, W., and Nanus, B. *Leaders.* New York: HarperCollins, 1985.

Bensimon, E. M., Neumann, A., and Birnbaum, R. *Making Sense of Administrative Leadership.* ASHE-ERIC Higher Education Report no. 1. Washington, D.C.: School of Education and Human Development, George Washington University, 1989.

Birnbaum, R. *How Colleges Work.* San Francisco: Jossey-Bass, 1988.

Burns, J. M. *Leadership.* New York: HarperCollins, 1978.

Gibson-Benninger, B., Ratcliff, J. L., and Rhoads, R. A. "The Implications of a Democratic Vision of Community College Leadership." Paper presented at the Annual Meeting of the Council of Universities and Colleges, Minneapolis, Minn., Apr. 1995.

Hilosky, A., and Watwood, B. "Transformation Leadership in a Changing World: A Survival Guide for New Chairs and Deans." Paper presented at the International Conference for Community and Technical College Chairs, Deans, and Other Organizational Leaders, Reno, Nev., Feb. 1997.

Kouzes, J. M., and Posner, B. Z. *The Leadership Challenge.* San Francisco: Jossey-Bass, 1991.

Mellow, G. O. "The Role of the Community College Chair in Organizational Change: Chaos, Leadership and the Challenge of Complexity." Address given at the Mid-Atlantic Community College Chair Conference, Blue Bell, Pa., Oct. 1996.

Myran, G., Zeiss, T., and Howdyshell, L. *Community College Leadership in the New Century.* Washington, D.C.: American Association of Community Colleges, 1995.

O'Banion, T. *A Learning College for the 21st Century.* Phoenix: Oryx Press, 1997.

Rost, J. C. *Distinguishing Leadership and Management: A New Consensus.* Paper presented at the Organization Development Network National Conference, San Francisco, Oct. 1985.

Rost, J. C. *Leadership for the Twenty-First Century.* New York: Praeger, 1991.

Welch, G. "Seasoned Chairs and Deans Can Learn New Tricks." Paper presented at the International Conference of the National Community College Chair Academy, Phoenix, Feb. 1996.

Zaleznik, A. "Managers and Leaders: Are They Different?" *Harvard Business Review,* Mar.–Apr. 1992, pp. 126–135.

ERIKA YAMASAKI is publications coordinator for the ERIC Clearinghouse for Community Colleges and a doctoral candidate in education at the University of California, Los Angeles.

An annotated bibliography on midlevel managers in community colleges is provided. It includes previous studies and descriptions of professional development programs.

Sources and Information on Midlevel Managers in the Community College

Elizabeth Foote

Midlevel managers in community colleges, whether they are called deans, chairs, or administrators, are responsible for training and supervising staff, assigning faculty duties, maintaining course syllabi, handling registration, recruiting students, and attending meetings. As several of the preceding articles conclude, chairs are essential to the daily operation of these colleges.

The materials reviewed in this chapter reflect the current ERIC literature on midlevel managers in the community college, including research studies, advice for managers, and leadership training. Most ERIC documents (publications with ED numbers) can be viewed on microfiche at approximately nine hundred libraries worldwide. In addition, most may be ordered on microfiche or on paper copy from the ERIC Document Reproduction Service (EDRS) at (800) 443–ERIC. Works preceded by an asterisk (*) are journal articles that are not available from EDRS. They may be acquired through regular library channels or purchased from one of the following article reproduction services:

Carl Uncover: http://www.carl.org/uncover/, uncover@carl.org, (800) 787–7979
UMI: orders@infostore.com, (800) 248–0360
ISI: tga@isinet.com, (800) 523–1850

Research on Midlevel Managers

Because midlevel managers are so important to community colleges, several research studies have been done to assess their job satisfaction, coping strategies, and personal characteristics.

Coats, L. T., and others. *FIRO B: Analyzing Community College Department Chairs' Effectiveness.* Paper presented at the Twenty-Fifth Annual Conference of the Southeastern Association for Community College Research, Panama City, Fla., Aug. 5–7, 1996. 26 pp. (ED 406 999)

A study was conducted to explore the relationship between the interpersonal behavior of community college department chairs and the assessment of their leadership effectiveness by department faculty. The study population consisted of 30 humanities and social science chairs at fifteen Mississippi community colleges, as well as 171 faculty members at the colleges. Element B from W. C. Schutz's Fundamental Interpersonal Relations Orientation (FIRO) was administered to the chairs to assess their interpersonal need orientation, while the Departmental Evaluation of Chairperson Activities for Development (DECAD) questionnaire was administered to the faculty members to determine their perceptions of chair effectiveness. Study results included the following: (1) in faculty ratings, 64.2 percent of the chairs were categorized as effective and 35.7 percent as ineffective; (2) there were no significant differences between effective and ineffective deans with respect to expressed inclusion, expressed control, received control, expressed openness, and received openness; and (3) significant differences were found, however, for the variables of perceived inclusion and wanted inclusion, with effective deans showing a need to maintain and establish interaction with others. Recommendations for policy changes and further research are included.

*Jones, D. R., and Holdaway, E. A. "Expectations Held for Department Heads in Postsecondary Institutions." *Alberta Journal of Educational Research,* 1995, *41* (2), 188–212.

A survey examining the managerial, academic leadership, and advocacy roles of department heads in a community college, a technical institute, and a university in Alberta (Canada) revealed substantial variation among roles for the three institutions and the need for administrative skill development appropriate to different stages of service. Includes questionnaire.

*Miller, M. T., and Seagren, A. T. "Strategies for Coping with Job Challenges in the Community College Department: A Comparison of Chair Perceptions by Work Experience." *Community College Journal of Research and Practice,* 1997, *21* (5), 493–500.

Describes a study of three thousand community college department chairs to identify and prioritize strategies used to cope with job-related challenges. Indicates that top strategies were related to relations with business and industry, maintaining the chair position, and internal departmental operations. Discusses implications for future research.

Murray, J., and Murray, J. "Job Dissatisfaction and Turnover Among Two-Year College Department/Division Chairpersons." In *The Olympics of Leadership: Overcoming Obstacles, Balancing Skills, Taking Risks.* Proceedings of the Fifth

Annual International Conference of the National Community College Chair Academy, Phoenix, Feb. 14–17, 1996. 8 pp. (ED 394 579)

Research shows that turnover in managerial positions can cost an organization from five to twenty-five times an employee's monthly salary. Although some turnover is inevitable, many times it is caused by employee dissatisfaction with the job or its conditions, and this dissatisfaction is often directly attributable to stress resulting from role conflict or ambiguity. This is especially relevant to faculty in educational institutions who experience demands to perform many discrete tasks. Further, the stress factors felt by faculty tend to affect chairpersons to a greater degree. Dissatisfied employees who remain on the job tend to be unproductive and to reduce the productivity of others, while dissatisfied department chairpersons can have disastrous effects on the morale of a department or division. Research has shown that the administrator's role is more important than environment, structure, and institution type in accounting for performance of the department. Research has also found, however, that the chair's position is fraught with role conflict and ambiguity. Because the quality of a college is determined by the quality of the departments and administrative behavior, the levels and causes of job satisfaction among chairpersons must be investigated and addressed.

Quinley, J. W. *The Use of Influence Tactics Among Mid-Level Managers in the Community College.* AIR 1996 Annual Forum Paper. Presented at the Thirty-Sixth Annual Forum of the Association for Institutional Research, Albuquerque, N. Mex., May 5–8, 1996. 22 pp. (ED 397 750)

A survey investigated the extent to which midlevel managers in community colleges used influence tactics. Survey respondents (N = 208) reported on a variety of influence behaviors, categorized into nine influence dimensions (rational, consultation, inspiration, ingratiation, legitimating, exchange, coalition, personal, and pressure). Analysis of responses revealed that, on average, rational persuasion, consultation, and inspiration appeals were moderately used; ingratiating appeals and legitimating tactics were used occasionally; and exchange tactics, personal appeals, coalition tactics, and pressure tactics were very seldom used. Except for legitimating tactics, all influence dimensions differed significantly in frequency of use by organization direction, defined as directed toward coworkers, subordinates, or superiors. Personal characteristics and college size were not strong correlates of influence tactic use. This community college population used influence more often than a comparison corporate population, though the rank order of use by influence tactics was almost identical. Possible confounding aspects, such as underreporting of tactics perceived to be self-serving, are addressed.

Seagren, A. T., and others. *Academic Leadership in Community Colleges.* Lincoln: University of Nebraska Press, 1994. 176 pp. (ED 373 810). Not available from EDRS. Order from University of Nebraska Press, 312 North 14th Street, Lincoln, NE 68588–0484; $15.

Drawing from a national survey of nine thousand community and technical college department chairs in the United States and Canada, this book offers insights on the personal characteristics, responsibilities, challenges, and strategies of chairs. Chapter One provides an overview of the study, including information on its rationale and purpose, instrument development, the population surveyed, and research design and procedures. Based on responses from approximately three thousand chairs, Chapter Two offers a profile of the individual demographic characteristics of the respondents, and their prior experience, type of appointment, and future goals. Chapter Three focuses on the characteristics of instructional units and their campuses, providing information on number of students and faculty, instructional focus, degrees offered, and instructional programs provided. In Chapter Four the chairs' beliefs and values are examined with respect to curriculum, students, mission, access, admissions policies, and relationships to business and industry. Chapters Five through Seven relate chairs' perceptions of the importance of their interpersonal, administrative, and leadership roles; of such tasks as faculty selection, provision of feedback, budgeting, professional development, and communication; and of administrative, leadership, interpersonal, and personal skills. Chapter Eight focuses on job challenges for the coming five years, while Chapter Nine deals with chairs' perceptions of selected strategies in relation to these challenges. Chapter Ten deals with selected institutional and personal characteristics and their relationship to responses. Chapter Eleven offers concluding comments and recommendations for future research.

Advice for Midlevel Managers

Several authors have offered advice to midlevel mangers to help them perform their duties.

Arismendi Pardi, E. J. "Development of a Handbook for Department Chairpersons at Orange Coast College." Ed.D. Practicum, Nova Southeastern University, 1997. 72 pp. (ED 405 923)
    A project was undertaken at California's Orange Coast College (OCC) to develop a handbook that would delineate the duties and responsibilities of department chairs at the college. To determine the appropriate design elements and content of the handbook, the relevant literature was reviewed, formative criteria were established and validated, and current administrative handbooks from all the colleges in Orange County were analyzed. Once the handbook was developed, a summative review of the final product was conducted. Results suggested that the handbook needed to include essential information for chairs to perform the duties and responsibilities of their positions adequately and ethically, and that to be effective it must be practical and specific. It was also concluded that a handbook must be developed with the audience in mind to ensure that it is written at a level targeted for the primary audience. Recommendations for implementing the new handbook at OCC included the fol-

lowing: (1) it should be presented to the college for adoption; (2) it should be forwarded to all the colleges in Orange County; (3) it should be reviewed, updated, and revised annually; and (4) the annual update should include input from department chairpersons who use the handbook. Contains twenty-eight references. Appendices provide the criteria used to develop the handbook, descriptions of faculty members involved in the formation and evaluation of the handbook, and the new handbook.

Gmelch, W. H. *Five Skills for Becoming a More Effective Team Leader.* Paper presented at the Third International Conference for Community College Chairs, Deans, and Other Instructional Leaders, Phoenix, Feb. 23–26, 1994. 12 pp. (ED 368 412)

Although 80 percent of all administrative decisions are made at the department level, many community college department chairs accept their positions without a clear understanding of the demands or training in leadership skills. It is critical to a productive department, however, that chairs possess the leadership skills to shape their departments into academic teams. Developing a team attitude requires passion, commitment, and continuing communication with faculty and staff. Specifically, research shows that a collective team climate requires the following characteristics: (1) clearly stated and agreed-upon long-term goals, (2) actively involved team members and shared management authority, (3) openly shared information with participative decision making, (4) a constructive approach to resolving conflict with attention to individual interests, and (5) top-priority attention to individual growth and self-development. Rather than doing everything for the department, effective team leaders share management activities by providing direction, strengthening relationships, and encouraging mutual respect. In addition, faculty members should be encouraged to excel in scholarly endeavors at their own initiative, while support staff should be challenged to set their individual goals in line with departmental goals. Chairs should establish an open climate of shared information in which conflict leads to collaborative solutions.

Hilosky, A., and Watwood, B. "Transformational Leadership in a Changing World: A Survival Guide for New Chairs and Deans." In *Walking the Tightrope: The Balance Between Innovation and Leadership.* Proceedings of the Sixth Annual International Conference of the Chair Academy, Reno, Nev., Feb. 12–15, 1997. 8 pp. (ED 407 027)

New academic chairs and deans can assume their new challenges with less frustration if they understand the essential elements for developing a culture of proactive change. One key concept is transformational leadership, in which leaders employ idealized influence, inspirational motivation, intellectual stimulation, and individualized consideration to achieve results. It is also important to understand that change is a process, not an event; is accomplished by individuals; is a highly personal experience; and involves developmental growth. Chairs and deans will be called upon to play many roles, including (1) change leader, incorporating characteristics of transformational leadership; (2) administrative manager, focusing on daily operations rather than innovation; and (3) college professional, or mentor, guiding faculty through team building and professional development. Studies have shown that deans and chairs are instrumental in implementing change at their institutions, with 80 percent of decisions at universities made at the departmental level. A study of the role of community college chairs in the change process found the following seven concepts for effective change: (1) the president should set the tone by employing visionary transformational leadership, (2) individuals should feel empowered, (3) teams should be used, (4) there should be effective methods for data collection, (5) there should be a focus on quality, (6) the college must be able to respond to change, and (7) constituents should be satisfied with college services.

Hoffman, S., and others. "Teaching and Managing: Conflicting Roles of the Department Chair." In *The Olympics of Leadership: Overcoming Obstacles, Balancing Skills, Taking Risks*. Proceedings of the Fifth Annual International Conference of the National Community College Chair Academy, Phoenix, Feb. 14–17, 1996. 10 pp. (ED 394 594)

Community college department chairs are called upon to be colleagues, peers, managers, and teachers, with duties and responsibilities that are usually far more complex and demanding than any college document can convey. As a result of the demands of the position, department chairs may experience role conflict or strain. Role conflicts are contradictions between roles that individuals feel because the expectations of one role are incompatible with the expectations of another. Chairs are expected to participate in the budget development process, course scheduling, faculty and administration representation, student advising, conflict resolution, personnel issues, and public relations. The effects of chair role conflict include personal and health problems, stress, and loss of family time and personal support systems. Although there are no guaranteed strategies to resolve role conflict, recommended techniques include the following: (1) develop chair networks for support, (2) survey department faculty for input, (3) perform and share with department faculty serious constructive evaluations, (4) avoid feeling that all decisions must be made on the spot, (5) employ effective time management skills, and (6) leave problems at the office.

Watwood, B., and others. "Managing Organizational Change." In *Walking the Tightrope: The Balance Between Innovation and Leadership*. Proceedings of the Sixth Annual International Conference of the Chair Academy, Reno, Nev., Feb. 12–15, 1997. 8 pp. (ED 407 017)

Based on studies comparing leadership in two rural community colleges undergoing change and on examination of the management of change at Maryland's Allegany College, this paper presents a conceptual framework and model for managing organizational change. First, a framework is presented for understanding the role of the community college chair in organizational change, suggesting that chairs should exercise visionary transformational leadership in their departments, empower others, make use of teams, maintain a focus on customers and quality, and ensure that meaningful data is collected. The framework also points to two expected outcomes of these strategies: institutional innovation and constituent satisfaction. Next, implications of the framework are described, stressing the important roles of both presidents and chairs in dealing with change, the importance of staff development for quality, and the need to balance instructional and administrative duties of chairs. Finally, a model for managing organizational change is provided, including the following four components: (1) conceptualization, or recognizing the different parts of a system as a whole, which may best be accomplished through cross-college representation on committees; (2) active, two-way communication; (3) commitment by leaders to organizational goals to gain the commitment of stakeholders; and (4) the creation of management systems and support services dedicated to managing change and monitoring progress in the change process.

Leadership Training

As this volume emphasizes, many training programs are available to midlevel managers. The following documents describe a few of them.

*Anderson, J. "Leadership Training Initiatives for Community College Administrators: A Focused Synthesis of the Literature." *Community College Review,* 1996, 24 (4), 27–54.

Provides a description of leadership training initiatives specific to the needs of community college leaders. Focuses on the development and organization of programs as well as their common elements and unique factors. An appendix lists initiatives identified in the research.

*Gibson-Benninger, B. S., and others. "Diversity, Discourse, and Democracy: Needed Attributes in the Next Generation of Community College Leadership Programs." In J. C. Palmer and S. G. Katsinas, *Graduate and Continuing Education for Community College Leaders: What It Means Today.* New Directions for Community Colleges, no. 95. San Francisco: Jossey-Bass, 1996.

Argues that graduate programs for community college leaders should help students understand democratic models of leadership and should recognize the leadership potential of all faculty and staff. Proposes that the programs should be based on a cultural model of organizations and on a relational model of discourse and communication.

*Hankin, J. N. "The Door That Never Closes: Continuing Education Needs of Community College Leaders." In J. C. Palmer and S. G. Katsinas, *Graduate and Continuing Education for Community College Leaders: What It Means Today.* New Directions for Community Colleges, no. 95. San Francisco: Jossey-Bass, 1996.

Outlines issues and concerns that should be addressed by graduate programs for community college leaders to help prepare them for the real world. Reviews concerns related to dealing with nontraditional students, developing meaningful curricula, learning conflict resolution skills, using technology to improve instruction, and solving other managerial concerns.

Runnels, A., and Mpinga, D. "Mentor Magic: Implementing a Successful Mentoring Program for New Chairs and Deans." In *Walking the Tightrope: The Balance Between Innovation and Leadership.* Proceedings of the Sixth Annual International Conference of the Chair Academy, Reno, Nev., Feb. 12–15, 1997. 7 pp. (ED 407 018)

The Institute for Academic Leadership Development is a two-semester practicum experience designed to help community college administrators gain leadership experience through the development and implementation of an Individualized Professional Development Plan (IPDP). The IPDP is designed to help participants gain knowledge of self, capacities for judgment and communication, interpersonal skills, understanding of power and politics in colleges, and the capacity to interpret personal actions. North Lake College in Texas implemented a mentoring program to accept a participant from the institute. The participant maintained constant communication with the mentor and was appointed as dean-in-training at the college for the two semesters. The mentor's role was to share information, answer questions, create opportunities, and advise the participant. Their relationship was based on the following strategies for academic leaders: focusing on innovation and change, being proactive rather than passive, concentrating on decisions, involving as many members as appropriate in decision making, and building on strengths and seeking assistance in areas of weakness. Key elements of the program included good communication between the mentor and participant, strong feedback, the opportunity to work with a broad variety of specialties, the opportunity to reflect on the experience, and flexibility.

*Vaughan, G. B., and Gillett-Karam, R. "ACCLAIM: A Model for Leading the Community." *Community College Journal,* 1993, *63* (6), 20–23.

Advocates an approach to community college leadership based on community-based programming. Describes North Carolina State University's Academy for Community College Leadership Advancement, Innovation, and Modeling (ACCLAIM) and its components, which include continuing education, fellows program, information development and dissemination, and university involvement.

ELIZABETH FOOTE is user services coordinator for the ERIC Clearinghouse for Community Colleges.

INDEX

Back Issue/Subscription Order Form

Copy or detach and send to:

Jossey-Bass Inc., Publishers, 350 Sansome Street, San Francisco CA 94104-1342

Call or fax toll free!

Phone 888-378-2537 6AM-5PM PST; Fax 800-605-2665

Back issues: Please send me the following issues at $25 each

(Important: please include series initials and issue number, such as CC90)

1. CC _____

_____

_____

$ _____ Total for single issues

$ _____ Shipping charges (for single issues *only;* subscriptions are exempt from shipping charges): Up to $30, add $5^{50} • $30^{01}–$50, add $6^{50} $50^{01}–$75, add $7^{50} • $75^{01}–$100, add $9 • $100^{01}–$150, add $10 Over $150, call for shipping charge

Subscriptions   Please ❑ start   ❑ renew my subscription to *New Directions for Community Colleges* for the year 19___ at the following rate:

❑ Individual $57   ❑ Institutional $107

NOTE: Subscriptions are quarterly, and are for the calendar year only. Subscriptions begin with the spring issue of the year indicated above. For shipping outside the U.S., please add $25.

$ _____ Total single issues and subscriptions (CA, IN, NJ, NY and DC residents, add sales tax for single issues. NY and DC residents must include shipping charges when calculating sales tax. NY and Canadian residents only, add sales tax for subscriptions)

❑ Payment enclosed (U.S. check or money order only)

❑ VISA, MC, AmEx, Discover Card #_____ Exp. date_____

Signature _____ Day phone _____

❑ Bill me (U.S. institutional orders only. Purchase order required)

Purchase order #_____

Name _____

Address _____

_____

Phone_____ E-mail _____

For more information about Jossey-Bass Publishers, visit our Web site at:
www.josseybass.com   **PRIORITY CODE = ND1**